D1349284

Humanity, Terrorism, Terrorist War

Humanity, Terrorism, Terrorist War

Palestine, 9/11, Iraq, 7/7 . . .

———

TED HONDERICH

To John with all
good wishes
from Ted
8 Mar 07

continuum
LONDON • NEW YORK

Continuum International Publishing Group
The Tower Building, 11 York Road, London SE1 7NX
80 Maiden Lane, Suite 704, New York NY 10038

www.continuumbooks.com

First published 2006

British Library Cataloguing-in-Publication Data
A catalogue record for this book is available from the British Library.

ISBN: 0–8264–9116–2 (hardback)

Typeset by Kenneth Burnley, Wirral, Cheshire
Printed and bound in Great Britain by MPG Books Ltd, Bodmin, Cornwall

Contents

To

Freddie Ayer, Alastair Hannay,
Timothy Sprigge and Johnny Watling

Our Questions

Was the founding of Israel in Palestine in 1948 right or wrong? What about what has happened there since the 1967 war of enlargement? How was the terrorist attack of 9/11 on the twin towers of America right or wrong? What of our following war in Iraq, a freedom secured but so many dead? What of the horror of the day of 7/7 in London? Was the horror of what happened in the subway trains and the bus, like that of 9/11, itself a proof? And what of right and wrong with more of the same that is to come? There *is* more to come.

Let us think of these things together. Let us, if we can, come to agree on argued judgements about them. They are thought to be connected, a series of related events. Let us anyway come to our own different judgements after listening to one another.

The questions of right and wrong are close to questions about the moral responsibility and the moral credit of people involved. Indeed the question of who is to be held morally responsible for something *is* a question of whose wrong it was – or the question of to what different extents it was the wrong of more contributors than one. This question of responsibility, of who needs to change or be changed, is of plain and immediate importance. But our fundamental and common concern is right and wrong, justification or the lack of it, what was permissible or obligatory and what was neither.

And hence, of course, right and wrong now. Nothing is ever only about the past. Indeed you can say *nothing* is about only the past. History, at the very least, is about present curiosity, present feeling. Recent history is almost always about present decision, present action.

In our societies we are well supplied with judgements, proposals and words, very often just enunciations of words, by our democratic politicians and those who speak with them. These words in answer to our questions are known and familiar, a kind of litany, and we hear them as if in a dream or some other suspension of judgement. We can do a real thing as well, which is to think and feel, think and feel for ourselves.

To give our own answers to the questions of justification with respect to Palestine, 9/11, Iraq, 7/7 and more of the same, and of moral responsibility, and of what is to be done now, will also be to give one more answer. To come to argued judgements in response to particular questions is necessarily and inevitably to do what has a general implication, or rather to do what derives from a general view. You cannot look at a thing, even a group of things, in isolation.

For a start, you will have to worry about being inconsistent, about being in self-contradiction, thereby cancelling your own propositions, in fact having no thought at all. So, in addition to thinking of the three questions of this time, we will be thinking of the general and fundamental one of right and wrong in the world, sometimes said to be timeless. You can also call this the question of humanity, decency or justice. In fact we will start with it. This will not be an introduction to what follows, but the construction of a foundation and structure for it.

A Division of Labour, Philosophy's Part

With all of our questions, including the general one, there is a division of labour. This is certainly so with the question of the conflict between the Palestinians and Zionism – with Zionism taken as being not something a little vague, but as the justifying, founding and defending of the state of Israel within more or less its original borders, those of 1948. There is a division of labour, too, with the different question of the Palestinians and neo-Zionism, the latter being the enlarging of Israel since the war of 1967 into still more of the land of Palestine, with all that this has entailed and may entail for the Palestinians.

There is also that division of labour about right and wrong, maybe just about the proof of wrong and getting rid of irrelevancies, with the terrorist attack by airliners on the twin towers and the Pentagon in the United States on 11 September 2001. Did the awfulness of it that gripped a nation settle the question of the nature of the attack and what to do?

So with the connected war by the United States and Britain in Iraq that began in March 2003. Was this war somehow like the terrorism of 9/11? Did it have justification anyway? That would not depend on the sincerity or general decency of the leaders of those countries, Bush and Blair. It would not actually depend on the truthfulness of the second of them, the leader who followed his leader. Even if he was not a man attached to truth, not capable of seeing its value, he might have been right.

So too is there the division of labour with the attack on three subway trains and a bus in London on 7 July 2005. Of what moral relevance, what relevance to right and wrong, if any, was the fact that the British Army had been engaged in the killing of greatly more of a people with whom the terrorists identified? Of what relevance, as a newspaper article asked a week later, was the fact that the British prime minister put his own people at risk in the service of a foreign power?

Historians, including historians of population, have a part to play in the question of Zionism and the Palestinians and the question of neo-Zionism and the Palestinians. How many Palestinians and how many Jews were there living in Palestine in what times? In Iraq, there are other questions for historians. How many people have died in the war and its aftermath, and how? Were those killed by the American and British forces, like those killed by the other side, fried or torn to death? Is that what missiles and rockets do? To turn to 9/11 and 7/7, and a harder question, has religion always served causes more real than itself? Has it been about desires for *this* life?

There is also a role for inquirers into international relations, first those who bring a power of knowledge and judgement to their work.

They may not be in university departments of international relations. The professor of linguistics Noam Chomsky is the exemplar in our history. Some of the labour of right and wrong also falls to good journalists, and not just preparatory work. What were the feelings, the attitudes to us, of those in Iraq we said we were freeing?

So too, you can think, are there parts with large questions of justification for partisans and propagandists, persons on a side, maybe well beyond self-doubt. They make some contribution to progress towards moral truth, towards what we can have of that kind – even if their commitment to it, and to truth itself, is weak or treacherous. John Stuart Mill argued along those lines, about the value of the expression of all opinions, however outrageous or appalling, in that foundation document of liberalism, *On Liberty*.

No doubt others can claim a part in the labour of trying to see what is right or wrong in general and then in Palestine and with those three things that have come after it, and, to say the very least, have something to do with it. Lawyers come to mind. Politicians too can claim a part in the labour of inquiry, I suppose, anyway some of them. They have got people to listen to them, which is some kind of certification. Political theorists can claim a part too. It is democracy that we are told we are bringing to Iraq.

Economists can help. What money has gone and goes from the United States to Israel, and what has it done and what does it do? International lawyers also claim a part, as you will be hearing more fully in a couple of minutes. So too do religious persons, some of them Islamic clerics, some of them rabbis, some of them American fundamentalists with what is kindly called a simple faith in the Bible.

Rowan Williams, the Archbishop of Canterbury, the leader of the Church of England, is less simple on his subject of how faith might begin to think and feel its way through such nightmares as 9/11:

> Even vile and murderous actions tend to come from somewhere, and if they are extreme in character we are not wrong to look for extreme situations. It does not mean that those who do them had no choice, are not answerable; far from it. But there is sentimen-

tality too in ascribing what we don't understand to 'evil'; it lets us off the hook, it allows us to avoid the question of what, if anything, we can *recognise* in the destructive act of another.

Does that help a little? Could be. Do you recognize yourself a little in a 7/7 bomber?

In the division of labour with respect to all the questions of right and wrong, philosophers have the possibility and maybe the obligation of a large part. The philosophers I have in mind have as their historical exemplars David Hume in Scotland and Immanuel Kant in Germany in the eighteenth century, and Charles Sanders Peirce in America in the next century. Descartes in France, I guess. Their thinking is a little underdescribed as analytic in a wide sense of the term.

It is a general logic. That consists in a clarity about things that most often is analysis of things rather than any other kind of understanding, and consistency and validity in thinking and arguing about them, and a generality that also makes for a completeness. With this logic comes a scepticism and balance, and should come some self-doubt. It would be mistaken to say that the historians and others do not aspire to and sometimes achieve this logic. But it is not and cannot be their preoccupation. They have other things to do.

There is a second reason for philosophy's part in the division of labour. The general question of right and wrong and related questions have been and are the principal subject of that part of philosophy that is moral philosophy or ethics. It is a strong and rich part of philosophy.

It has in it distinctions our leaders pretend not to know, or which are overlooked by them, or which they have never known. It knows that the connection between the wrong of a killing and someone's moral responsibility for it is not simple. Moral philosophy knows, say, that to hold a leader morally responsible for something, or to have a part in the responsibility for it, is or may be to do a certain thing – seek to stop him from doing more, maybe worse, and not to be fixed only on his past. It knows too the connection and also the want of connection between such virtues of character as sincerity in an action and whether it is right.

It may be that no kind of proposition of morality that comes up with Palestine, 9/11, Iraq, 7/7 and what is to come is news to moral philosophy. Every kind of proposition has been the concern of prolonged inquiry and dispute. Demands of consistency, of single rather than double standards, have always been defended and examined. It would be as ignorant to put aside this reflection as to put aside, say, such works as *The Population of Palestine: Population History and Statistics of the Late Ottoman Period and the Mandate*.

Something the same is to be said of that part of philosophy that is political philosophy. There has been more superiority about it as against moral philosophy in what perhaps are the most relevant places, good philosophy departments in universities. Political philosophy is moved by actual political commitments. Some political philosophy tolerates the intolerable. But in fact there has often been real inquiry in political philosophy, different in kind from the declamations of elected democrats and the ideology in the partisan think-tanks on the web. To have a hold on this philosophy is to have a hold on something useful.

Again it is the more or less analytic part of it that I have in mind rather than, if you will allow me to say so, the recent French philosophy. The latter is rather more creative, another kind of thing. It can see the *reality* of 9/11 as being an image prefigured by a dream. That is interesting, but it seems to leave out the dead. Whether or not much of analytic political philosophy can get into a short inquiry, to know some of it is to know that it is necessary to proceed with caution. Say about democracy.

Still, what we are about to engage in, neither my part nor yours of our joint inquiry, can aspire to quite the detachment of Professor McCarthy's book on the population of Palestine. Or, if there is one, an entirely independent military history of the war in Iraq from 20 March 2003 up to 1 May 2003, when Bush said the war was over but in fact there were still many people to be killed. Or the detachment of what unloaded journalism there is on the personal histories of the 7/7 bombers.

The logic of philosophy, or the aspiration to that logic, when it is pursued within moral and political philosophy generally, or with respect to such questions as those we are about to consider, finds itself engaged in a kind of *advocacy*, an advocacy of arguments and judgements. A decent philosopher dealing with moral and political questions, as has been remarked before now, is in a line of life higher than that of a trial lawyer, but not out of sight of that line of life. If there is what can indeed be called moral truth, it is not ordinary truth. Desire gets into it.

There have indeed been and there are indeed philosophers who are only partisans of the sort mentioned earlier, not loyal to either factual or moral truth. I trust it is possible to distinguish between them and those other philosophers true to their calling, advocates more constrained by moral truth and by truth. In our conversation I hope to be among them.

To which needs to be added one thing with respect to your expectations about my part in our inquiry. What you are about to read is not the final communiqué on four particular subjects and a general one from a World Congress of Philosophy. It is the communiqué of one of us, no nearer to being a majority than any other, further away than a lot, but trying to make use of our joint tools.

Negotiation, International Law

Despite all that, might it be that we should proceed in our philosophical reflections on our subjects by way of some body of thinking or some practice separate from philosophy?

What of the idea, associated with pacifism, and estimable and goodly persons, that peaceful negotiation is always to be preferred to violence? And so it follows that the right answer in Palestine will be reached if both sides renounce suicide bombs and helicopter gunships, and just talk instead? And that all of 9/11, war in Iraq and 7/7 were terrible mistakes for this simple reason?

The general principle against violence can hardly be serious. Is the woman in the very course of being raped to try to reason with the rapist if she can hit him over the head and stop him? Am I only to *exhort* him to stop? It is impossible to believe, more generally, that the right answer is guaranteed always to result from negotiation rather than anything else. The general principle against violence has the consequence that engaging in war, including a war started by the other side, has never been right – and presumably, until more is said that is going to transform the principle into something else, that having a police force has never been right.

The general idea has the consequence, to come closer to one of our subjects, that only slow negotiation is right for a people who have some violent means of trying to stop what has already begun, their actual destruction. It cannot be, either, that we should have arranged a meeting in Geneva rather than fought to halt the Holocaust when that horror was being carried forward.

It cannot be said that when the weak negotiate with the strong, they can count on reason to make them equals. Or that the strong will always negotiate, as distinct from pretend to negotiate while going on using their strength somewhere else, on the ground. Something else that comes to mind is that a nation wholly in the wrong may plan and act to make it impossible for its victims to have a hope of redress except by violence – and then condemn the violence very effectively.

No doubt there are times, even many times, when the right thing to do is to negotiate. It is inconceivable that it is *never* right to do otherwise, never right to be violent. This is an idea, by the way, that shares a kind of pious simplicity with some other ideas, a simplicity that defeats them. We know already that large questions of right and wrong do not have easy answers. If they did, we could have got them by now. An easy answer is wrong.

The one we are contemplating, by the way, against all violence, is not really the one given by Gandhi, the great exponent of civil disobedience against the British Empire in India. As the admirably cool American philosopher Virginia Held reminds us, and as the cool British political thinker Bhikhu Parekh confirms, Gandhi did not believe that a good cause should restrict itself to civil disobedience if that had no hope of success. If he said it is best of all to resist oppression by non-violent means, he also said it is better to resist oppression by violent means than to submit.

Can we get better help in our inquiry by starting from the work of some of those other labourers already mentioned? Some professors of international law may bravely say we ought to be guided by it. We ought to be guided by the conventions, principles, precedents, treaties and customs of international law, for example about declaring war or the conduct of war.

The idea faces large difficulties. One is that our inquiry is into what is right or wrong in Palestine, and what has been right or wrong in Iraq and elsewhere, not into what is legal or illegal. Patently there is an entire distinction between what is right and what is legal, a gulf. It does not depend on the fact of moral awfulnesses in the legality and law of the past, say slavery. The distinction is untouched too by the fact that what is legal is sometimes also right. It is also untouched by anyone who takes rights seriously, and does not fully distinguish legal from moral rights.

What is actually right, patently, is not itself what has been made into law by someone or come to be law as a result of increments of decisions, precedents or pressures. When we ask such questions of right and wrong as we are asking, we simply are not asking questions to be settled by lawbooks and the like. We simply do not mean, in saying something is right, just that it is the law of the land, or of lands. Was the Holocaust legal in Germany, by the way? Judgements and agreements as to what is right are prior to and give rise to law, and are the stuff of arguments for and against existing laws, and are what changes those laws. Necessarily, therefore, the moral judgements and agreements are different, and are what is fundamental, however they are expressed and whatever they may be called.

So if we were to proceed by way of the conventions, principles, precedents, treaties and customs of international law, we would not be dealing with our question. Nor could we thereby avoid our question. It would not go away. In particular, we could not avoid the question of whether the judgement of international law on Palestine is right, or on 9/11, Iraq, or 7/7.

There are other reasons for not starting with international law as a body of canons, principles and so on. One is that it is not settled what it is. That is to say, in fact, that in part it does not exist. More particularly, it is in crucial parts open to something all too close to self-interested invention. With respect to Iraq, one thing was clear. There was no agreement between the leaders of the invading nations and their lawyers and others as to whether the war was legal. The rest of the world saw that the invading parties and their few supporters were making up law. In fact it was absurd to speak of *law*. It is no surprise but an insufficient concession that a good note on international law, by a reputable jurisprudent who is no firebrand, ends with the admission that this law is peculiarly open to change through *fait accompli*, by national states prominent in shaping and appealing to its rules, principles and institutions.

Do you have the idea, about international law as it stands, that whatever it is, however much of it there actually is, it is closer to right than anything else, whatever may be right? Do you say a lot of hard thinking has gone into it? Do you note that it has in it a principle of self-defence, which must be right whatever misuse has been made of it? Do you remember that it has in it the Geneva Conventions on the conduct of war, very likely of great value at least sometimes?

Well, it is true that international law has in it some or other entirely defensible part or parts, rather like the part of the ordinary criminal law of a particular society that has to do with murder and other offences against the person. As you can say, it is moral as well as legal. It has been a good help in some circumstances. You can also say that the existence of some law is one argument, of lesser weight, for the wrongness of what it prohibits. But that falls well short of a general recommendation of international law for our purposes.

To have such a general recommendation, for a start, you would also have to think up and say a lot more against an unbroken line of well-armed sceptics. They run from Thrasymachus in Plato's *Republic* to philosophers of law and indeed lawyers today. They have the theme that justice is the will of the stronger, or too close to that. And anyway it is absurd to say that something-legal-you-know-not-what, some or other parts of a thing, is to be depended on for a rightness-you-know-not-what. That might pass in a speech to retiring magistrates, but not in the real world. We need to know the parts, and, more than that, why they are defensible.

Do you say that the question we are considering is not separable from a harder one, the question of whether some part of international law owed to or supported by democracies is right? Well, it is totally unclear what law it is that you are recommending. If it is law consistently supported by democracies, there may be very little of it indeed. But in fact you're changing the subject from law to democracy. We will come to that.

Do you say something along the following lines? That the rightness of the law, including international law, is actually not what matters – what matters is that it *is* the law? There just is that fact. This is pretty common talk, but unclear. You can of course say the thing, maybe to the retiring magistrates. What you can't do is what you seem to be trying to do, despite a contradiction. You can't both get rid of the question of the law's moral decency and also imply that somehow the law is a justified imperative. And if you are not implying some such thing, you have wandered into the wrong discussion. Our subject *is* right and wrong, the main subject in connection with four things and some more, the subject that no one can avoid and in fact no one does.

So put aside the idea that we can decide what is right and wrong in Palestine and elsewhere by starting with our international law as it is – the canons, customs and so on. The law will be of some use, but not decisive. What of the more general idea of going by what is called *the rule of law*? That is the idea, presumably, of always going by some or other body of international law, as distinct from what may be supposed to be the body of international law at a particular time.

This is in fact a greatly *less* persuasive idea than going by what international law we have. To what is being proposed, if you think of it, there is a simple reply. We cannot suppose that there is *no* conceivable body of law, however monstrous, such that we should abide by it rather than break it. It cannot possibly be true, despite a certain amount of ancient wisdom to the contrary, that any rule is better than no rule. It cannot possibly be true that every conceivable law should be kept in order to serve or support the whole institution or fabric of the law.

To this rule-of-law idea there are also the previous objections to beginning with international law as we now have it. In thinking of going by whatever rule of international law, we necessarily have to open the question of moral decency. In this case we cannot begin to get any help from the law for the special reason that we have no single body of law to consider. And there is the other problem in a special form. How can we be guided by we-know-not-which of various alternative bodies of law, no doubt inconsistent ones?

UN Resolutions

Another and different idea having to do with international law may come to mind. You can take international law to consist in more than the conventions, principles, precedents, treaties and customs. It has become ordinary to take resolutions passed by the United Nations as being part of or even basic to international law. The legality of our 2003 war in Iraq was considered mainly in terms of such resolutions. But there is more hope in thinking of resolutions on Palestine. There was more agreement, to say the least. And, as you can suppose, Palestine has the importance of entering into our other three particular subjects.

Since the 1967 war of enlargement, Israel has been the subject of something like 65 resolutions of the Security Council of the United Nations. There have been resolutions against the project of taking still more of the land of Palestine than Israel acquired originally, in 1948 – the project of neo-Zionism. Certainly there is reason to distinguish this project, as we already have and as the world does in several ways, from the founding and continuing defence and the justification of the existence of Israel within its original borders. There is also reason for appropriating a name for use in our inquiry and speaking of this latter cause as Zionism, whatever the connections and continuities between Zionism and neo-Zionism so defined.

The resolutions have condemned, censured, deplored or regretted the actions and policies of neo-Zionism, and called on it or urged it to cease and give up the actions and policies. The resolutions have had to do with the occupation of still more of the land of Palestine, killings, massacres, racism, making Palestinians into refugees, the destruction of their homes, the taking of their water, the establishing of Jewish settlements, imprisonments, deportations, harassments, and other violations of what are called human rights.

These resolutions have almost all been passed by majorities of between ten to one and fourteen to one in the Security Council, which has in it fifteen nations as members. The overwhelming majorities have included four permanent members of the Security Council, these being China, France, Russia and the United Kingdom, and also very many nations who have had temporary membership of the Council.

The single dissenting vote, by the United States on behalf of Israel, has been a veto. It has left the resolutions in absolute existence as condemnations or whatever – what else could a fourteen-to-one vote be? – but without force as a result of the United Nations Charter, the organization's founding constitution. The resolutions have issued in no action by the United Nations. So too, on account of the constitution, with a great many resolutions of the General Assembly against neo-Zionism.

There have been no such United Nations resolutions against the Palestinians. The short story is that the United Nations has consistently condemned neo-Zionists rather than the Palestinians. But it has been prevented from taking effective action by its constitution and more particularly by the use of the constitution by the United States.

It will be impossible to inquire into right and wrong in Palestine and ignore these resolutions, this fact of human judgement. It is a judgement by massed nations, judgement as good as unanimous, judgement by what it is reasonable to call the representatives of the human race. Certainly the fact is of such a size as to overwhelm imputations against them.

As already remarked, it is clear enough that in some of its parts international law approximates more to a kind of agreed morality. One of those parts, indubitably, is the resolutions against neo-Zionism we are considering. When they are taken to have made Israel into a pariah, as they have been, they are not being regarded merely as pieces of legality.

But if here we are a lot closer to our subject-matter of right and wrong, and if some may think that the international consensus makes neo-Zionism *prima facie* wrong, that is not nearly the end of the story. It remains the case that there are those who take the resolutions to be wrong. There are simpler Americans who do so. There are also Americans of dual loyalty, in fact neo-Zionists. They take or declare the resolutions against neo-Zionism to be one-sidedness, double standards, blindness, international politics, or of course anti-semitism. That is not a fact likely to give much pause to an actual moral philosopher, even an American one. But that they can do so does point to other things.

We need to remember that what is legal, even if its character as legal rather than moral is indefinite, is at bottom no more than legal. Further, the legality of the fourteen-to-one votes is no greater than the legality of the veto-right of each of the five permanent members of the Security Council. We also need to be restrained by the fact of which you will eventually hear a bit more. A UN resolution brought about an international embargo including medicines that resulted in very many children dying in Iraq. The worth in argument to you of some UN resolutions must be less if you are picking and choosing among resolutions.

There is a larger matter. Most readers of this book, I suppose, including many brave Israelis and many Jews elsewhere who have membership in a splendid Jewish tradition of moral and political perception and fortitude, an exemplary realism, will be affected or more likely have been affected already by the fact of the Security Council resolutions. A philosopher not more than affected by them is a philosopher who has become a partisan or worse. The resolutions are in fact one kind of moral data, if not one of several more important kinds. But they call out for at least a kind of clarification, a clarification that could possibly affect the simpler and other Americans.

On what general moral ground or grounds do the resolutions against neo-Zionism rest? Do they have a consistent ground that shows them to be consistent with other resolutions – and with the absences of other resolutions? Do they have a basis that makes clear why there are no resolutions against Palestinian terrorism? What is the fundamental principle that recommends the resolutions – and which they recommend? Or, if you like, into what outlook, view or vision of what is right do they fall? Into what conception do they fall of how our human lives together ought to be?

The resolutions in themselves do not answer this question. They do not answer this question despite their implications of morality, forceful implications. They are not near to completing an inquiry into right and wrong in Palestine. They are not near to giving a full and systematic answer to the question, an answer that has the strength of logic. They are not an answer hard for a people to put aside, even an ignorant or a self-deceived people. Even if the American people as a whole were to come to be properly informed and hence enabled to start thinking, they might not stop with the resolutions.

The situation is no different with 9/11, Iraq and 7/7. That your feelings are stronger with all three, or with two of them, perhaps overwhelming, does not in itself make these cases different in the given way, does it? It's not UN resolutions that give us answers to right and wrong.

Human Rights

Shall we try to go forward by way of another United Nations fact? Shall we look to human rights, presumably the principal charter of them that exists? That is the Universal Declaration of Human Rights, adopted and proclaimed by the General Assembly of the UN in 1948.

It guarantees everyone's life, liberty and security of person. Also everyone's freedom from fear. All of us are also to have freedom of movement and to be able to leave and return to our country or territory. There is to be no exile. All are to have the right to a nationality, and not to be deprived arbitrarily of their property. All are to have a standard of living adequate for their health and well-being. There is to be no discrimination or attack on honour and reputation. There is to be no racism.

The declaration also contains more general propositions. One concerns a problem that arises with any collection of rights. That is the problem of conflicting claims with respect to the rights, or indeed actually conflicting rights. What happens when my security conflicts with your freedom from fear? And so on. What the declaration says is as follows.

> In the exercise of his rights and freedoms, everyone shall be subject only to such limitations as are determined by law solely for the purpose of securing due recognition and respect for the rights and freedoms of others and of meeting the just requirements of morality, public order and the general welfare in a democratic society.

Another general proposition of the declaration needs remembering. In a subordinate *if* clause, much debated and not accidental, it allows for departures from the rule of law, indeed for what is called rebellion:

... it is essential, if man is not to be compelled to have recourse, as a last resort, to rebellion against tyranny and oppression, that human rights should be protected by the rule of law ...

It might be argued that the implicit right to rebellion is reinforced by the absence in the world of what is called for by a further general proposition. That thing is a social and international order that actually defends all the rights and freedoms of the declaration.

Let us also note one other general proposition about rights, in this case in the United Nations Charter. It speaks of territories whose peoples have not yet attained a full measure of self-government. It asserts that

the interests of the inhabitants of these territories are paramount.

The territories are to be supported by the United Nations in the development of their self-government or independence. It is not the interests of those who administer or seek to swallow the territories that are paramount.

There is no doubt that the Declaration of Human Rights and the United Nations Charter have on balance been of service to us, more particularly to many of the world's victims. Like UN resolutions, the declaration and the charter cannot possibly be ignored, whatever self-interested use has also been made of them. You could start with them in working out an answer to our questions about Palestine, Iraq and the terrorisms. Is this the best place to start, however? In fact, how much of a place is there to start from?

It is clear enough what human rights are. They evidently share something with their historical predecessors, what were called *natural rights*. Human rights are what give rise to and justify bodies of national and international law, the positive law at which we have been glancing that is laid down, enacted or ratified by a national state or states. Above all, human rights are what give rise to and justify legal rights. They are what can be appealed to in judging and seeking to change national or indeed international law and the legal rights in it. In short, human rights are surely moral rights, or some moral rights. So we are not definitely in the wrong ballpark.

And what is a moral right to something? Well, for someone to have a legal right to something is for them to have the support or legitimation of national or international law, to the extent that the latter exists. For someone to have a moral right to something is for them to have a different support or legitimation in the rightness of their claim. They have the support, evidently, of a moral principle that is somehow fundamental, binding, irrefutable, justified, established, accepted or the like. That is to say, at least implicitly, that the person who has the moral right has the moral support of other people, at least some other people. This matter of moral rights will also be of importance in another context or two.

To start from the collection of human rights in the charter, from the right to life through the right to a nationality to the right to reputation, is not to start from a ragbag, as some have said. But evidently it is to start from a mixed bag. You can be excused if you ask what the bag itself is. What brings these rights together? What unites them? What sums them up? You can look at the preamble to the declaration and the rest of it without getting an answer.

It cannot be that *nothing* sums up these rights, that nothing unites them. We would have a greater understanding of them if we had an answer to the question. We would have an idea of their ranking. They are not of absolutely equal weight, are they? Your life itself is more important than my reputation, isn't it? If we had a summary, we would also be on the way to knowing what can be added to the listed rights and what cannot. No rights of women are mentioned, by the way. There is nothing to the effect that they share the rights of men.

There is a related but greater difficulty that arises in trying to settle the matters we have on our agenda, Palestine, 9/11, Iraq, 7/7 and so on, by recourse to the declaration. Something like a principle would not only be enlightening and a guide but is also just necessary. This has to do with the fact, already noticed, that claims to rights and indeed rights themselves come into conflict.

We have it in the first quoted passage that people are to have those rights and freedoms *that are in accord with the rights and freedoms of others*. Which are they? That is fundamental. We get no answer at all, none. We are here at the centre of moral and political philosophy, indeed of morals and politics, and what we find in the Charter is a hole. There is no more help in the bare reference in the same passage to *morality*. What morality? Nor is there much help in the references to general welfare and public order in a democratic society. What kind of democratic society, for a start?

Do you have the idea that somehow we do not need a principle in order to settle the matter of Palestine by way of the declaration? Some audacious philosophers have said there are no principles at all in morality, but then some philosopher can be found who has said anything you like. Leave that. Do you have the idea that we can get some half-idea or tolerable idea of a principle by somehow adding up the mentioned rights and freedoms, beginning with the right to life? Well, let's have that idea please.

Palestinians believe, certainly, along with most of the rest of the world, that the declaration supports them in their struggle with neo-Zionism. That proposition as it stands seems to me obviously true. It is in accord, you can say, with the spirit of the declaration. Some Palestinians may believe, too, that they can state a principle that will help them, a principle that gives general content to the declaration's sentences about rights. There is another fact, however. It is that neo-Zionists believe or at any rate declare otherwise.

There are conflicting judgements too with Iraq. Some say it has simply been a war for human rights, those of the Iraqis. There is disagreement too about 9/11 and 7/7. That we may take those attacks to be monstrous does not remove them from the world of reasons, the world in which reasons for and against are heard. That is the world in which we are, reader.

Is there not a more persuasive way of proceeding, perhaps what turns out to be a way that will leave neo-Zionism with less possibility of belief or declaration? And so with the defenders of the terrorisms and maybe the Iraq war? It needs saying that a general principle in morality cannot be a magic wand. It will not make things simple, turn darkness into light, leave us with no problems. But it will help a lot and do a lot, won't it?

After all, it is pretty close to true that *generalization*, so disdained by some, is the essence of inquiry, the stuff of science, even the nature of intelligence. You see what is true or right in a particular case by comparing it with others. And it isn't just a slew of particulars you come to depend on, but what you have had to make of them.

Something else in the declaration needs noting – the quoted general proposition about tyranny and oppression, by which we need to understand ethnic cleansing and a good deal more. What is allowed, most relevantly to our concerns, is that people may be *compelled* to have recourse to armed resistance and the like, to killing, as a last resort. What is to be understood by this large concession?

Clearly it is not that the people in question are subject to compulsion by other people holding guns to their heads. It is not that they are left no more room for decision than you are when somebody really does hold a gun to your head, or when you are in the real grip of a psychological compulsion. Rather, what is and must be meant is that the people in question are subject to an overwhelming reason for armed resistance. It is a reason, not merely a cause, that is in question.

What is that reason? It will have general application, of course, like all reasons. Or, if you suppose, bravely, that the sort of reason in question is plain to see, what is it for it to be overwhelming? What makes a reason overwhelm others? It is notable that Palestinians claim to have overwhelming reason for their terrorism and that neo-Zionists deny it. There are these differences in Iraq too. They exist as well with the terrorist horrors of 9/11 and 7/7. For all these adversaries and for us to think about this matter effectively, we need to do something else.

As you know already, we need to come to a general view, a generalization about right and wrong, a generalization that also includes something so far not much mentioned, or not mentioned explicitly. To think about what ought to happen is necessarily not only to think about a goal, but also of how to reach it, what is to be said for certain means.

There is an assumption in thinking of what ought to happen by way of international law as canons, principles and so on. It is that the end we have is to be pursued, so to speak, by conventional means. In fact it is to be pursued by way of law. A question arises of what recommendation this has as against alternatives. Despite what is said of rebellion, is there a related legalistic assumption in thinking about Palestine by way of UN resolutions and human rights?

A more complete answer to our questions will be something that has in it general propositions about right and wrong means to an end, about general policies and practices. Necessarily the answer will have in it some argument for these as against others. They will not have to do with just legality and the likes of rebellion, but with means to well-being generally.

Just War Theory

You will have heard from a decent newspaper, or a pulpit, of the *just war theory*. It came up with Iraq, as it has with almost all wars.

It had a beginning in the medieval Catholic Church. The philosopher Augustine was a founder of it. It is still being elaborated in the philosophy department of the University of Notre Dame and also, in part, with a quite different goal, in the philosophy department of the University of Haifa. It is better to speak simply of *just war theory*, however, since there certainly is no settled and definite thing that is *the* just war theory. There is a collection of ideas that are given different understandings and weights by different people and traditions.

A just war in the intended sense is evidently a justified war, a war that is right, a war that it is not wrong to engage in. Possibly a war that it would be wrong not to engage in. The term 'just' with its legal association obscures this a little, for whatever reason or out of whatever motivation. But there is no doubt that what is in question is not merely a somehow legal war. What we are promised here is in fact an answer to the question of what wars are right, what wars ought to be permitted by or called for by international law. A just war, conceivably, could be against some international law.

The ideas in just war theory are traditionally divided into necessary conditions to be satisfied in going to war, and then necessary conditions to be satisfied in conducting the war. We need not attend to this division. It is artificial, partly for the reason that rightly deciding to go to war must involve thinking about how it can be waged. There is also the fact that one idea, about what is called proportionality between a thing done and what is to be gained from it, turns up both in the recommended thinking about the whole prospective war and then the thinking about possible actions or operations in carrying it forward, say carpet-bombing of German cities in World War 2.

A just war is a war that (1) has a just cause. Such a purpose or intention has often been spoken of as self-defence in the plain sense. To engage in self-defence in this sense, you have actually to be attacked first. This self-defence is a response to somebody else's actual aggression, coming over your border with tanks or launching missiles. The just cause here, also, may be said to be peace. But, very differently, a just cause is also now spoken of in just war theory as something else – a defending of human rights, or the defending of a decent way of life. A war with such a purpose or intention can be *started* by you. You can be the aggressor, anyway technically speaking.

A just war (2) has to have a probability of succeeding in its cause. There must be a reasonable chance of this. The war must not be hopeless. It must not look like being pointless suffering.

It also (3) has to be taken forward by the right entity or persons. Originally these were limited to national states or the leaders of them. Now, however, the right entity or persons can conceivably be a resistance movement or insurrection or the leaders of such things. The anti-apartheid movement in South Africa was a recent thing that made the change necessary.

So, depending on how you understand terrorism, it is a possibility that terrorism and terrorists can be engaged in a just war, or anyway in just terrorism. It seems that what we are considering, at least until more is said, is a theory of just war and maybe just terrorism, maybe Palestinian suicide bombing and the attacks of 9/11 and 7/7.

Partly in order to avoid the matter of the definition of terrorism, to which we shall come later, let us stick to thinking and speaking of war in an ordinary sense. A just one and what is done in it, as you have heard, must be (4) proportional. Considered as a means, the war as a whole must be somehow proportional to the end to be gained. The means must in some sense not be too costly, not be excessive. So with actions, operations and tactics in the war.

The war (5) must in some way not involve the killing of innocents, non-combatants or the like.

Also, it must (6) be a last resort. It must be taken only after peaceful means of settling a dispute have proved ineffective.

To all of which is added, anyway typically, that a just war (7) involves the right intention, having to do with its just cause and nothing else.

That sketch of just war theory may persuade you of what has to be granted, that you could usefully start here in thinking about Palestine or Iraq, and maybe 9/11 and 7/7. I agree. What you would be starting with, however, is a collection of problems. Perhaps it is not too much to say you would be starting with a mess of problems.

With respect to requirement (1), the just cause of war, does the idea of self-defence in the plain sense have to be enlarged, as indeed it has been by some thinkers, recently by those two thinkers who have been our national leaders in connection with Iraq, so as to include pre-emptive self-defence? If so, what is the line between that and other aggression? More seriously, since some line can always be drawn, what would be the justification of exactly that line? In particular, where in just war theory do we find that justification?

That is not the only trouble with the propositions about just cause as they now are. We already have it that a just cause for war may be other than self-defence, plain or pre-emptive. A just cause may be such as to justify an attack that is not pre-emptive, in fact an attack that the other side can with reason call aggression. This could be an attack to preserve human rights, where the violation of them has not been by means of war. A just cause could be an attack to prevent ethnic cleansing, maybe an attack to defend a way of life. Could a just cause be a holy war? You will agree that we have to hear a lot more about these things.

More than that, since not all ways of life can possibly be defensible, we will need a general way of deciding on ways of life. So too with conflicts or seeming conflicts between human rights.

To come to requirement (2), certainly it makes good sense to say, as a first try, that a war must not be futile. There is something fundamental there. But can men or an army of them fight for the future without hope of keeping their own lives? That is not unknown. Nor has it been disdained. Such men have been venerated and not thought to be crazy. They may be again.

What of the need for a war to be (3) conducted by the right persons? Does this in fact turn out to be something different, the need for it to have a certain cause? Once you make the critical departure from the original requirement, limiting the right persons to national states, it seems you may get that conclusion about a just cause. Perhaps the right persons are those not aiming at private gain, not aiming at anything like a business corporation's gain? But is it the case that *any* cause of the leaders that is public-spirited, so to speak, is all right? Would that include freeing a people from what their leaders say is the dirt of a minority living among them? Here again we need an account of just causes.

When it is said (4) that something must be proportional to something else, in what way is it to be proportional? It would be kind to exclude the idea that does turn up in some just war theory, that the war or the operation is proportional to the *guilt* of the other side. Here, it seems, as with a proportional or deserved punishment, the proportional war or operation may actually turn out to be understood as the right one. There will be the result that argument for its rightness is merely circular, a begging of the question at issue.

Better, is the proportionality to be thought of in terms of costs to human rights? Those human rights that conflict and for which we lack a way of deciding between them? Also, is the prospect of an American way of life for another people a candidate for what is to be compared with 100,000 deaths in terms of possible proportionality? If that question offends you or makes you suspicious of your guide in this inquiry, you can have emollient ones instead. We certainly do need some principle or method for comparing two things in order to see if they are proportional or not. What is it? Is it possible to proceed with this doctrine without such a thing?

With respect to (5), who are the innocents? Children, presumably, but who else? What is this innocence? Are all non-combatants innocent? All civilians? Also, in what way must a war not involve killing innocents? Could it be that a just war is one in which there is reasonable or well-based foresight or anticipation or probability-judgement that no innocents will be killed? There have been no such wars, no real ones. Neither World War 1 nor World War 2 was conceivably a just war in this sense.

Clearly there is room for thought about (6) the requirement that there be no alternative to war. There is also room for thought about the difficulty of judging that matter. On one side of a conflict there may be an industry devoted to falsehoods about past alternatives in negotiation not taken by the other side, about the first side's negotiations having been true negotiations rather than false or pretended. But, putting aside this, do we maybe have to live with the difficulty? Is there a question of the necessity of judging in conditions of uncertainty?

Finally, does a war cease to be justified when it turns out that it is taken forward with (7) the wrong intention? Are we not to support an army that may be in process of saving 100,000 lives or maybe 1,000,000 lives because its commanders and their government have impure intentions? Maybe impure intentions with bearable bad consequences that can be anticipated, but bad consequences dwarfed by the anticipated saving of the lives?

Just war theory has had a lot of intelligence put into it. It neither justifies all wars that count as according to international law nor necessarily condemns all wars that count as against this law. It gets beyond legalism. It raises natural questions that no one can avoid. They will get separate attention in what follows in this inquiry. We will be coming back to the matter of killing innocents, for example, and the necessity of judging.

Just war theory's difficulties can be summed up in a certain way. How are we to be guided in answering these questions that plainly come up in connection with the requirements (1) to (7) for a just war? We need guidance and thus consistency and balance, not momentary intuitions. If the requirements as we clarify them pull in different directions, as indeed they may, and we need to amend or develop them further in order to bring them into consistency, by what means shall we do that?

A fundamental principle is needed, isn't it? At any rate something like that. It may well be that the theorists of the just war have attempted answers to the many questions it raises, indeed the questions we have noted. I have not heard that they have transformed it by giving it a foundation not known to be part of its history.

A fundamental reason is also needed for something else, isn't it? How else are you to choose between competing claims, some of them at least persuasive, in the four things that are international law and negotiation, the UN resolutions, human rights, and just war theory? Just to pick and mix items without a reason would be to have nothing informative to say to yourself or anybody else on behalf of one collection as against any other.

The Politics of Reality

Just war theory, and also the conventions, treaties and what-not of international law, and UN resolutions and human rights, are still condescended to by some American, English and other professors and students of international relations. In the past many more prided themselves on having a sharper eye for the nature of the world of nations. Their attitude was and is shared by a good many politicians, diplomats and corporation executives themselves. They too take themselves to see what they take others of us to obscure by our unworldliness, innocence or hope.

In place of this, to use a plain word, they put a cynicism, or maybe naïveté, the attitude that everybody and every group is entirely governed by selfishness or self-interest. They may add, by implication, that there is something to be said for this, or anyway something to be said for what they may call not trying to renounce membership in the human race. Along with this is likely to come superior or denigrating utterances about mere value judgements, subjectivity, emotive meaning, relativity in morals, something being true for you but . . . , and the like.

We hear, as a result, that we are to guide ourselves as nations by the politics of reality, known in the past as *Realpolitik*. It has long been associated with Bismarck, Germany's Iron Chancellor towards the end of the nineteenth century. It is often defined as politics based on realistic and practical considerations rather than moral or ideological ones, or considerations about human rights or whatever. It is a calculating self-interest. It is also disbelief about the stated or seeming positions of other parties, and a readiness to use violence, go to war, quite possibly illegally.

It is not easily separated from the politics of power, *Machtpolitik*, relating to other parties only in terms of their power, paying attention to their demands or situations only to the extent that they have power. It goes entirely beyond an idea in arguable moralities. This is that a person or a country or a people can to a certain extent concern itself with itself, look after itself, as others do – there is this useful division of labour.

A first thing to be said about all this is that nobody can avoid being subject to moral judgement by trying not to be guided by it in his or her own life – or succeeding. Neither can any group or nation do so. Further, no person or nation ceases to be open to moral judgement because somebody else, say a regiment of academics, half-says they are not.

Moral judgements on any X, for a start, are at bottom a set of thoughts and feelings pertaining to X. They come to a kind of approval, maybe of an end or goal and a proposed means to achieving it, maybe of the end or goal but definitely not a proposed means. The thoughts and feelings do not evaporate because they may not suit X or may simplify the life of somebody studying X. A side of our life, indeed more than that, maybe the bottom of our life, does not cease to exist.

There is something else. We, at least the great majority of us, most certainly do not stand in a relation of only pure self-interest to the rest of the world. For a start we *are* affected by famines, tsunamis and submerged cities. Nor have our governments always been purely self-interested. To suppose otherwise is to suppose that no war has ever been entered into for other reasons than what our vulgarians call the bottom line – in this case national profit or loss, or more likely profit or loss for one part of the nation, a part on top.

Indeed one of the curses of the thinking of political realism, and indeed a curse of our age's thinking about so much, is the simplicity that there are events and there are their causes. There is the lighting of the match and there was its striking. It is as madly forgetful to think that large human events have single causes or conditions as it is madly forgetful to think dryness and oxygen had something to do with the lighting of the match. *Of course* self-interest enters into the explanation or causal circumstance of a nation's relations to the rest of the world. *Of course* that is not all that does. Do the remaining realists among scholars of international relations not read any books outside their departmental libraries?

There is a general and fundamental fact that lies behind the proposition that we are not simple in being self-seeking. We as a species are rational in a certain minimal sense. That is to say that we have reasons for what we do – good, bad or indifferent reasons. Reasons are by their nature general. If R is a reason for doing something in this situation, it is also a reason for doing it in any other identical situation, and, more important, it is of relevance and a constraint in similar as against identical situations. We are also alike in another way, which is that we share fundamental desires. These two facts are much of what makes us a species. These two facts, about reasons and desires, of which you will be hearing more later, tie each of us in a way and to an extent to others.

Do you suppose, incidentally, that it is always possible to find a reason that serves one's pure self-interest or one's nation and commits one to nothing else? Certainly I cannot produce such a reason for something's being done, why it ought to be done, just by saying 'I say so', or 'America says so'. That carries a troublesome implication about suchlike sayings by others. They can say a thing like that in Iraq too, and in Palestine, and in Saudi Arabia. They could have said it too in a street or two in Leeds when they were planning to put the bombs on the subway trains on 7/7 in London.

Furthermore, if it were possible to find a so-called reason devoid of such implications, that would be no help. We can see through false reasons. We already know what sorts of reasons other persons and groups really have. We can see when their reasons are not what they say they are, but are about their desires shared with the rest of us.

But it is not just that no person, people or state can escape moral judgement by not being guided by it themselves, and that we do have some sympathy for others, however limited, and that no ordinary person or people escapes the general implications of their reasons, and that our nature as a species lies behind this fact.

If we come to have leaders sufficiently dim, crass, callous or vicious to have escaped this membership in a species, there is still something else that stands in the way of their embracing what at first seems to be the politics of reality and the politics of power. The politics of reality and power can at first seem to be an obliviousness of decent moralities, one in particular of which you will be hearing. But in fact it would be self-harming for our leaders, however crass, always to ignore these moralities.

Sometimes to do so will simply not be rational, in another and more ordinary sense – it will not be an effective means to the end and one worth taking. It will not be such a means to the entirely self-interested end of the political realist. Rather, ignoring morality will give rise to resistance, opposition and attacks, maybe war, maybe terrorism. It must sometimes be that decent action, however amoral in intention, is what serves a country's self-interest.

So, putting all else aside, the politician of reality himself, and the rest of us, need to know what decency comes to, at any rate if there is some convergence on this, some agreement, as plainly there is. Even the absolute and unmitigated politician of reality cannot stay right out of morality. He needs to know about right and wrong, which is not to say that it is what he takes to be his own nation's morality. That is not of use to him here.

The point can be made in terms of dealing with unofficial terrorism, what is simply called terrorism ordinarily, as against official or state terrorism, of which distinction you will be hearing more. The New Labour Party in Britain, in its first years of government from 1997, made a lot of use of the line 'Tough on Crime, Tough on the Causes of Crime'. That, it said, summed up its right policy about juvenile delinquency, ordinary burglary and the like.

The line wasn't heard after 9/11, no doubt because of the prospect of a reply about the right policy on terrorism – tough on terrorism, tough on the causes of terrorism. But even our silent democratic politicians are aware that we need to think about the causes of terrorism. To do so necessarily is to get into the question of decency or rightness. You have to get into that even on the way to saying no terrorism ever has been defensible in any way at all.

One more reflection along similar lines. The politics of reality, you can think, starts by being patently inconsistent. That is, it does not grant the legitimacy, in some sense, of somebody else's self-interest. But then minimal or species rationality plays a part – the fact that we have reasons, and they are general. So an American politician can find himself seeming to be committed to the Chileans or the Russians or indeed the Iraqis just serving their own self-interest too. American politics of reality then adds to itself some moral or ethical proposition to try to distinguish itself consistently from *other* people's politics of reality. That is not easy.

Or the American politician makes the simpler addition that everybody, all countries and peoples, are engaged in the self-interest of the politics of reality. So it is fair and right that America should do so. This supposedly *fair politics of reality* is vulnerable to the proposition, among others, that all parties do not have the money or other power to act on their self-interest to the same extent, and hence that the fair politics of reality is in fact unfair, indeed monstrously unfair, as almost all of us agree. But the main point here is again that even the politician of reality needs to know *what* is decent. He needs somehow to be guided by that in his self-serving additions. He can no more escape the subject than those who write books about him.

Conservatism and Liberalism

We can contemplate a different step to what may be recommended as realism. Questions of right and wrong are the stuff of the real or ordinary politics in which we all have to exist – the large political traditions, of which a larger one is conservatism and another is liberalism. The politicians of parties in these traditions let us know often enough that something or other is right, sometimes using the very word, more often using some synonym that is less likely to evoke a challenge. Indeed, they let us know that something about Palestine is right, or wrong. We also hear about evil, a good deal about evil.

We can then turn first to the tradition of conservatism and see what we can find that may enable us to come to reasoned answers to the questions of Palestine, 9/11, Iraq and 7/7. What we will look for is aid to answers of the general kind we are pursuing. Those are answers that have the recommendation of the logic of philosophy – clarity, consistency and validity, and generality. Maybe being sceptical instead of credulous.

What we need to look for, then, is unlikely to be pronouncements that were the news of a day. Not what English journalism is always on the lookout for, the time's big idea. Rather, we need to look for whatever principles of judgement, stated or unstated, inform the tradition of conservatism, and perhaps can be put to use by us. We can also look for *the* principle of conservatism, which can also be called its rationale or best summary. There has to be such a thing.

Conservatism is the political tradition that has been typified in the past by the Conservative Party in Britain and the Republican Party in the United States. Is it to be understood as the political tradition that is against change but for reform? That was declared by Edmund Burke, MP, author of *Reflections on the Revolution in France*, in the eighteenth century.

The difficulty is that even the fortitudinous Burke failed ever to explain what he bravely and no doubt nervously called this manifest, marked distinction. It cannot be a difference between large and small alterations in things, since conservatism in its history, and today, is in favour of and committed to large alterations, maybe of some whole society, for example that of Iraq. Some conservatism is keen on altering the world.

It has often been remarked that the conservative tradition in politics is distinguished by being against theorizing and for experience. Burke devised good sentences against theorizers about natural rights and whatever else – those half-dozen grasshoppers under a fern who make the field ring with their importunate chink whilst thousands of great cattle, reposed beneath the shadow of the English oak, chew the cud and are silent. Burke got resolute support from the American John Adams, who gave attention to what had lately been named *ideology*. He said our more familiar words *idiocy* and *idiotism* are not sufficient to catch its reality.

One difficulty here is that the tradition of conservatism, being a tradition of some intelligence, is in fact itself quite full of theory. Much theory, actually, is attempted explanation, and we all like it and need it. Some conservative theory is about international relations, some of this being the political realism or *Realpolitik* at which we were looking. Also, you may remember hearing of the luminous sociology of the Third Way. That was the uncertainly guiding light of New Labour governments in Britain, of which it became very necessary to judge that they were actually conservative in nature.

To come on to something else, is conservatism informed by exactly a principle of opposition to the particular changes that are violent revolution, revolt, terrorism and the like? And of course the theory of them? If so, and if this line of thought is general and well developed, we may conceivably find ourselves benefiting from a well-grounded argument for a condemnation of Palestinian terrorism.

But there cannot possibly be such an argument in conservatism. The tradition itself has in fact admired, supported, paid for and not very covertly engaged in revolution itself. It has been for revolutions against the French and the Russian Revolutions. It has been for revolt against democracy in both Chile and Nicaragua. It has been for innumerable recourses to political violence. Depending on how you define terrorism, it has been for an awful lot of terrorism. That the fact needs reporting is a triumph of the great fact of convention in our societies, also the great fact of useful ignorance, of great use to some in our societies whether or not they set out to manufacture them.

An inquiry into the supposed and the real distinctions of conservatism does not quickly make clear its rationale or fundamental principle – whatever it is that issues in its commitment to some kinds of alteration rather than others, some theories and some revolutions rather than others, and so on. No rationale is evident in its other distinctions of enthusiasm for some freedoms, having to do with private property, and resistance to other freedoms, say those having to do with getting a job and greater democracy. It cannot be that its rationale is a principle of desert, people having or getting what they deserve, which collapses into a principle of unexplained rightness itself and anyway is open to anybody's use, on any side of a dispute.

You cannot move from here, reader, to the familiar proposition that conservatism is the politics of self-interest. Self-interest turns up in *all* political traditions, parties, movements and struggles. Neo-

Zionists and Palestinians are not without self-interest. What can be said of conservatism, rather, is something else. What it is necessary to judge of at least the Republican Party in the United States, and became necessary to conclude of the New Labour Party in the United Kingdom, is something else. Conservatism is the politics informed by nothing other than self-interest, whatever moral or moralistic talk goes with it. It is not ruled or informed by any discernible moral principle.

As such, plainly, it can give us no help with our questions. We may conceivably have a promising idea in this self-interest of *why* conservatism is by and large better disposed to the adversaries of the Palestinians than to the Palestinians, the explanation of this. We have no answer to the question of why we ought to join conservatives in this disposition, a general reason for doing so.

The view of conservatism as no more than a class or classes of people out for themselves gets dramatic support, by the way, from a close look at its leading philosopher of a little while ago, Robert Nozick of Harvard. The perfectly just or morally ideal society, he explained, is the one where all the good things in it have a certain history. They have a history in accordance with certain requirements.

Take an apartment in Cambridge, Mass., maybe near Harvard. Somebody mixed their labour with something to come to be the first owner of the apartment. If they aren't the legal owners now, they sold it or gave it to somebody else, who may have started a long chain of such transfers. If, along the way, somebody got hold of the place by squatting in it or by fraud, then that has been somehow rectified – things have been made what they would have been if the first two requirements had been respected.

Why is the society where everything is like this perfectly just? The short answer we get is that it is in accord with personal liberty. What is that? Obviously what somebody defends as a personal or other liberty is some freedom they think we ought to have, a freedom they take to be justified. Justified by what in this philosophy? No answer is even attempted. We have no idea at all why squatting in an apartment or taking it into public ownership is not justified. No idea of anything that justifies the self-interest or selfishness of some of us.

Notice, by the way, that in this perfectly just or morally ideal society, where everything is owned according to the historical requirements, an unlucky family could be starving to death. Nobody else and nothing else would have a moral obligation to save them. They would have no moral right to food. The only moral obligations and rights in this morally ideal society are fixed by who has legal ownership of what.

We can be less embarrassed for the human race if we turn our attention away from this thinking and feeling to liberalism, conceived as a broad tradition around the centre in politics, but one that has a large division within it. It is the politics of the centre that has much to do with what it calls individual rights. These may be the private property rights that are yet dearer to conservatives, or they may be rights of some strength to the necessities of life, maybe spoken of in terms of a welfare floor.

Here, as with conservatism, we find a collection of ideas and attitudes concerned first of all with life within one or another of our wealthy societies. Is liberalism yet more limited than conservatism to such a subject-matter? Still, one might expect the possibility of *some* light on Palestine from what is indeed one of the main ideologies of the modern world. It is very confident, after all, about its reasonableness, and takes itself to be more human than conservatism.

Liberalism had a beginning in that work already mentioned for its defence of the free expression of all opinions, *On Liberty*. In that much-studied book, John Stuart Mill set out to give a simple answer to the question of what the liberty or freedom of an individual should be – an answer to the question of to what extent an individual should be left uncoerced by either the law of a society or social pressures in it. His answer, or rather his answer the first time he gave it, was that

the only purpose for which power can be rightly exercised over any member of a civilized community, against his will, is to prevent harm to others.

That has a ring that has recommended it to many. It depends, after the ring, on what it is for one person to harm another. Can I harm you by refusing to join your union? By wanting your colony of flagrant gays out of my apartment block? By worsening your local school by sending my children away to a private one? By having a racist march near your mosque? By urging everybody to boycott your supermarket that has neo-Zionist connections?

Some have said that in speaking of stopping A from harming B Mill had in mind A harming just the legal rights of B. That has the unfortunate upshot that in a society with laws permitting slavery or torture, no slave-owner or torturer would rightly and justifiably be interfered with by state and society. There is also the upshot that we get no principle at all, but only very different useless instructions relative to different societies and legal systems.

Some have said that A harms B in Mill's understanding if A goes against the greatest happiness of the greatest number, the principle of the moral and political philosophy of utilitarianism. But it happens to be the case that Mill wholly subtracted even that degree of clear sense from the utilitarianism into which he was born. He elevated and spiritualized it. He never succeeded in saying, despite repeated efforts, what it is for A to harm B and thus to be rightly restrained or whatever.

John Rawls was the voice of liberalism or anyway *a* liberalism of the twentieth century. In *A Theory of Justice*, very long, he first asserted a principle of individual rights, also called liberties, including rights having to do with private property. This was to have precedence over a second principle, one of equal opportunity. And that second principle was to have precedence over a third. This was that a society has to have whatever socio-economic inequality, none at all or some or however much, that makes a worst-off class better off than it would be without that inequality.

Rawls, in *A Theory of Justice*, notoriously left the liberties vague. In his later writing, if the liberties were clearer, their rationale remained uncertain. His third principle, paid more attention than the other two, left it wholly unclear *what* inequalities are necessary to the end in question of making the worst-off class better off than it would be without the inequalities. Indeed, it was left open that 'necessary' might mean inequalities that are 'demanded by the best-off in America'.

It remains obscure what liberalism really comes to. Still more important, it remains more obscure what liberalism rests on. What is the principle that we might try to carry with us into reflection on our Palestinian questions? Does liberalism reduce to the vagueness of good intentions not carried into definition and resolution? Good intentions hobbled? What good intentions? The principle, by the way, cannot be what liberalism shares with different political traditions, and is not at all unique to it, which is some sort of commitment to democracy, a subject about to have our attention.

To linger for another minute, can it be supposed that even if Mill and Rawls and lesser lights are no specific help, we should take from liberalism some commitment to *freedom* to direct us in our inquiries? Well, one reply is a general thought about freedom. It is that when you are actually thinking about any freedom, rather than just orating about it, you need to ask what the good of it is.

We English who depend on trains to go and see our families are not keen on the property-freedom that was the privatization of our railway. Nozick did not like the social freedoms that went with ordinary taxation, since that taxation was regarded by him as forced labour. There was not a lot of good but rather horrific bad in Hitler's freeing Germany of the Jews. There is not a lot of good in freeing the state of Israel from those of its inhabitants who are Palestinians, or freeing Israelis from the effect of Palestinian votes.

Freedom will be getting our attention too, but, to stick to conservatism and liberalism, our result is clear. We do not get an aid to our inquiry from these persistent traditions. You may think that this was not to be much expected, since both are first of all about politics in one country. I do not agree with either of those points. But if you are right, we can anyway have the reassurance of having seen something of the extent to which conservatism and liberalism are without a more general application or relevance.

So we can agree on something. Either the two traditions are to be regarded as not having much relevance to our questions about Palestine and so on or they are to be regarded as having a relevance. On neither assumption do they produce the goods. On the second assumption, what is relevant is also a mere matter of self-interest or something so indeterminate as to be useless.

Democracy's Equality

The leaders of the democracies of the United States and the United Kingdom, Bush and Blair, said after 9/11 that they were absolutely clear in their own minds, as on so many subjects, about the great new fact of the world. It was a war of some kind between the good of democracy and the evil of terrorism. From this report of a Manichean conflict between light and darkness, various propositions about democracy could be sorted out. A couple will do.

One is that in any conflict between a democratic state and terrorists – terrorists as usually conceived – the democrats are somehow in the right. Not necessarily entirely so, maybe, but largely so. Although the democrats too are killing people, including innocent people, maybe killing very many more of them than the terrorists, that they are democrats makes a difference. So too does this make a difference to right and wrong in any conflict between a democratic state and a non-democratic state or a less democratic state, such as Iraq.

Another proposition is that with respect to a conflict between any national state whatever and terrorists as usually understood, or between any national states whatever, there is no better judgement of right and wrong than that of another democracy not itself in the conflict. Or, to speak differently and more clearly, we can take it that the judgement of an uninvolved or disinterested democratic state about what should happen with respect to a conflict with terrorists or between states will turn out better than any other judgement.

So we can see what is right and wrong in Palestine by going by our own democracy – by its party platforms or manifestos, speeches, elections, debates, conferences, policies and legislation. Presumably above all its speeches and policies on the subjects of Zionism, neo-Zionism, Palestinian terrorism, terrorism directly against us, invading Iraq, a new constitution for it, fighting on against the unwelcoming Iraqis, and so on.

The propositions are sides of what has to be taken to be the general and greatest recommendation of democracy. There has been a whole welter of recommendations of democracy. It has been justified as the political system whose citizens are sovereign, which is to say most free or most equal in their political experience, participation or consent, or where the people are likely to be benefited by economic freedoms, indeed free enterprise. It has been argued that they are likely to come to have characters or personalities of a superior kind. It has been argued that democracies settle questions within their own borders peacefully, and are unlikely to start wars. But what must be taken as the general and greatest recommendation of democracy, one that subsumes others, is something else.

It is that it *gets things right*, across the board – on domestic and foreign policy having to do with private and public enterprise, taxation, health care, war, foreign aid and whatever else. Or, to make the usual quick retreat to a safer position, it *gets things more right* than any other form of government. It gets them more right, or at least less wrong, or is more in the right or less in the wrong, than dictatorship, rule by army generals, other oligarchy, overt or official plutocracy, an empowered elite of whatever kind, a social or educational or intellectual ascendancy, a hierocracy or theocracy or excessively religious state – and also any leaders of a revolution, putsch, insurrection or terrorist campaign who have come into their leadership by other than a democratic election of our kind.

There has been a short answer to the question of why democracy gets things right or less wrong than these alternatives. It is that with respect to taking the right decisions for a society, and other societies, two heads are better than one, and a lot more heads still better.

Everybody having an equal say, freely bringing their own experience to bear, compensating for the shortcomings of others, produces the best upshot. This result of equality and freedom, as distinct from the experience of those two things by the citizens, is the general and greatest recommendation of democracy.

This will be the case, anyway, under conditions of something like wide public knowledge in a society and hence a knowledge-related capability of judgement. The assumption of knowledge and judgement, it has to be said, does face some difficulties. To see the difficulties, have a look at the newspapers that inform most heads, say the *Sun* in England or the *New York Post* in America, or listen to the news on small-town television or for that matter CNN. You can wonder often enough about the BBC too. But there is another possible answer to why democracy gets things more right.

The fact of everybody's being heard, or anyway a lot of people being free to be heard, may not involve decent pieces of knowledge resulting in better decisions. But everybody's being heard, or anyway a lot of people being heard, at least guarantees that very many wants or desires go into the society's decision-machine. Each of many people register a little effect, put in a little data. There is a lot of input. Other systems don't register everybody's wants equally. People don't get this chance in other systems. No doubt there is a problem of the worth or justice of the desires when they have to do with other countries, whose desires don't get into the machine, but let that pass.

As against these several short answers to the question of why democracy gets things at least less wrong, there has been the fuller explanation that is what you can call the traditional description of this form of government – itself a departure from the ancient mistake that democracy actually is government by the people. The traditional description, like others, brings in the two ideas of freedom and equality. Here, democracy is said to be government freely chosen by and freely influenced by all of the people rather than a few or a single class. More is added. Three propositions.

It is said that in a democracy the people freely choose governments in regular elections – choose the persons who actually do the governing and decide on the country's relations with other countries. And the people freely influence those governments between elections. The people are not compelled or constrained in this choosing and influencing of governments. There is this voluntariness with respect to a society's internal policies and its external relations, including relations of war and peace.

It is said, secondly, of course, that what happens in a democracy is choosing and influencing in which all the people are equal. There is universal suffrage. Each head counts as one and no head counts as more than one. That was put forward as being as large a consideration as that the people are free of dictators, generals, priests, leaders of an insurrection or the like.

Thirdly, we are reminded that the elected governments themselves proceed by free and equal majority vote. And, as needed to be added, their decisions are effective. The decisions are not made ineffective by somebody else or something else, say international corporations. The elected representatives in a democratic government would not be freely and equally deciding things if in fact they were not really the people deciding things.

That is the traditional explanation in its three parts of why democracy gets things right, or less wrong. But in fact it is given no longer, except by some politicians in public speeches and by the newspapers and television when they are not thinking much. Even our politicians, when they are off duty, not actually engaged in politics, now allow that another description of democracy, an up-to-date description, is true to our facts, more realistic. This has to do mainly with the matter of equality.

We hear from the up-to-date thinkers that there is not complete equality in the voting in a democracy, where that would be something very close to all the people having the legal possibility of voting – more people than in Florida, where enough people were denied the vote to secure the election of Bush for his first period of office. It has also sunk in on the up-to-date thinkers that there is certainly not complete equality among citizens in the effects of the voting.

The citizens do not have equal effects since many less than all of them do vote, often only about half, for whatever reason, and those who vote very definitely do not have the views of those who do not. Also, with respect to the unequal effects of the voting system, and as is well enough known, a winning party in a democratic election can be elected with fewer votes in total than the losing party. And democratic governments can have huge majorities in the assemblies with hardly more votes than the losing party.

These facts about our voting are familiar, indeed a little boring. They are also something else. They are very good reasons for giving up at least the traditional conception of democracy. By themselves, they stand in the way of at least the traditional assumption about equality, that the people make equal choices in voting.

There is also a fact much larger than any inequality among citizens with respect to just the voting. The larger fact has to do with the influencing of governments between elections and, quite as important, the influencing of what choices will be on offer at elections. This matter of influencing is indeed a much larger fact. It is such if we are engaged, as indeed we are, in considering why the answers to questions given by democracies, why the choices of democracies, are better than the answers and choices of other kinds of governments.

Thus the up-to-date thinking about democracy, as against the traditional thinking, is indeed that because of differences in influence and the other things there is *less than full equality*, or *less than ideal or total political equality*, in our democracy. Our politicians when off-duty and other personnel engaged in educating the public leave it at that, are not much perturbed by their new realism, and do not expect the public to be.

They are wrong in the extent of their qualification, wrong in the smallness of their revision of the traditional thinking. To start to see why, think first of something else, of an employment law or an employment practice that affects men and women, or maybe Protestants and Catholics. Suppose this law or practice secures that the men or the Protestants are limited to having only *100 times* more opportunity of getting a relevant job than the women or the Catholics. That would certainly not recommend the law to women, Catholics, or anyone thinking about effects of equality and inequality. It would be crazy. Or take a fact of educational opportunity for children in a neighbourhood – some having 100 times the chance of getting to a proper school, or of just learning to read. Or think of people dying of hunger, and giving some groups 100 times more food. 100 to 1 is no good. It is *inequality*, not equality.

To come still closer to our subject in hand, think of the members of a family deciding whether to sell the family house – where for some reason or other one brother has 100 times the power of decision of anybody else. Or think of a workers' union, where some members each have 100 votes, as against other members having one. Think of a university's decision to charge high fees that will exclude many would-be students, a decision where the members of the Department of Economics have 100 times the say of any other faculty members. 100 to 1 is no good in taking decisions. It is inequality, not a kind of equality.

Now come back to democracy and the up-to-date description. There are things to be added to what has been said of equality already, at the very least things to be made more explicit.

Robert Dahl of Yale University was an astute and maybe the best political theorist and scientist of American democracy. He wrote something about it half a century ago. It was that a university professor in such a democracy, himself a figure far from the bottom of any relevant scale, might have a thousandth or a ten-thousandth of the political freedom and power of a newspaper publisher like Luce, Springer, Hearst or Murdoch. Things are very definitely not different now. In fact there is *more* concentration of power of several kinds.

That is one proposition that needs to be added with respect to the unperturbing propositions of the revised description of democracy. It is not the only fact or kind of proposition about our democracy that needs to be added, and in fact not one of the large and really consequential kinds. Those are not just about newspaper publishers and other such leading and celebrated individuals.

In the United States, the tenth of the population with most wealth in fact has about 70 per cent of the total wealth in the society. The bottom tenth has none or less than none – it owes more money than it has. As for income, the tenth of the American population that has most in fact has about 30 per cent of the total income in the society, as against about 2 per cent of it for the bottom tenth. There are similar facts in such other countries as the United Kingdom. They never stop coming out, despite government promises and predictions to the contrary.

In this connection you may remember that there used to be Marxists. They wrote books like my old friend Jerry Cohen's *Karl Marx's Theory of History: A Defence*. You may have been like me in not needing the theory in question and its metaphysics to know the simple truth that economic power translates into political power, that money makes for votes in a lot of ways. So it may be easier for you too to hold on to that simple truth despite the decline of the mentioned theory. *Obviously* there is a strong connection between economic and political power.

Think of another top tenth of Americans, defined in terms both of most wealth and most income. They indubitably have more than 100 times the political power of the worst-off tenth, far more. The inequality has been underestimated or underguessed by me before now, by the way, but I have since then been more impressed by yet some more facts, smaller and larger.

One smaller sample has to do with the American elections to the Senate in November 2004, when Bush became president again, this time by winning. Of the eight Senate seats where there was no sitting incumbent, and thus a real race, winners officially spent an average of $9,473,789, much more than the losers. One consequence of such facts is a tremendous reduction in voter choice, a decimation of it. This is not about the losers. Ideas and options of potential candidates who cannot attract dollars and so do not run at all are never heard. No real reformer of health or corporation taxes is going to raise $9,473,789. He might get $100,000, and so he doesn't try.

Economists and political scientists have not got around to providing some less informal and more complete account of elections and money, let alone economic and political power generally. That is not really something that can detain or obstruct us, even for a minute. In matters of seriousness like this, it is a mistake, maybe dishonourable, to delay stating a clear enough fact until some professional body has got into action. You can argue that to delay is to go *against* intellectual principle and academic propriety. Both of these presumably have something to do with *truth*.

There is a larger fact of economic and political power that comes together with and in fact is not separable from the personal wealth and income inequalities within our societies. It is the pressure or constraint on our democratic decision-making by both international financial and trade organizations and international corporations and also by national-level public and private administrations, bureaucracies and corporations. It goes beyond an older connection between democracy and economic freedom or free enterprise.

This consortium of several sectors and levels has as its official concerns responsibility, stability, reciprocity and other means to economic progress. It has in it the International Monetary Fund, the World Bank, the World Trade Organization, and some hundreds of international and to a large extent supranational corporations. It also has in it the departments of commerce and trade and the like and the national corporations in each of the western or rather northern democracies.

In fact the consortium is a descendant of empire and colonialism. It is more commercial than economic, in ordinary senses of those words. It is now squarely within and perhaps the most consequential part of the political tradition of conservatism. Its real concerns are widely known. They are the preserving constraints on economic relationships that serve the interests of the northern economies, absurdly called free trade, the privatization of what was publicly owned and conducted, the ending of regulations serving public ends rather than profit, freedom for foreign investors in all economies, the reduction of government insofar as this does not affect the consortium's concerns. All of that comes under the heading of globalization and is as rightly spoken of in terms of the market, an American hegemony, and sometimes the political class.

It is not often enough said that the aim of the consortium is not truth. More generally, the aim of buying and selling is not and never has been truth. It is not and never has been what is right either. The aim of a market is neither truth nor what is right. Nor is there the slightest reason to think that buying and selling or the market produces more truth or more of what is right than would be produced by actually aiming at the truth or what is right. The aim of the consortium is indeed the strengthening and increasing of the means to business as usual and the returns from it.

It is worth lingering in this neighbourhood long enough to reflect that it would actually be an amazing fact about our behaviour and existence, one that would revolutionize or shut down whole university departments and decimate libraries when discovered, if it turned out to be true that the best way to achieve some great end, or indeed any end at all, say tying your shoe laces or organizing a drinks party or observing a religion or educating children or improving a nation's health or making war, was for nobody really to think about it, nobody to concentrate on that end.

We achieve things by having conscious desires, thinking about how to satisfy them, considering reasons for and against possible steps, experimenting, taking reasonable steps towards the goal. An opposite view, known as the Hidden Hand Argument for individual self-interest and a market, was owed in the first place to the eighteenth-century economist Adam Smith. David Hume should have been more careful in choosing his friends. No amount of repetition of the Hidden Hand Argument makes it other than a nonsense that is gratifying and of some use to people taken up with a line of life. No more do you get a decent society by not trying to get a decent society than you win a war by not trying to win the war.

In connection with democracy, the effect of the consortium is sometimes contemplated in terms of that part of democracy that is the taking of effective decisions by government, its actually making happen what it decides is to happen. Plainly the consortium limits this power and sometimes overcomes it. This is not our present concern. Our concern, rather, is the equality or inequality involved in the process whereby our governments come to judgements on Palestine, 9/11, Iraq, 7/7, and very likely will come to judgements on what is to come after those things.

It is indubitably the case that the consortium is a weight on pre-cisely the *judgement* of democracies – their thinking and questioning itself, that process of supposed equality or near-equality – as distinct from a constraint on their actions. This is the weight of a consensus. It is self-described as one of realism and an awareness of what is possible, which is to say of the supposed extent of the possible and thus of what is to be taken as necessary. What is necessary, in short, is the stability and continuity and the like, where the like includes law, negotiation, democratic means and so on. All of it in distinction from terrorism – terrorism as ordinarily understood – and from some war.

These many facts, from the boring ones about voting to those about the power of certain individuals and the wealth and income distributions in our societies, and then to financial facts about elections to the fact of the consortium, add up to an inequality in economic power that simply refutes the up-to-date description of our democracy. It is in fact dopey to say, as do those English and American politicians off duty, only that there is *less than full equality* or *less than ideal or total political equality* in our democracies. It is a matter of our conventions of idiocy, conventions born of self-interest and against truth and logic, that an English university professor can say, as one once did, that there is *approximate equality* in our democ-racies, that the political influence of one citizen is *not wholly out of line with* the influence of another, that there exists *tolerably similar* influence. I was the professor.

Our democracies, in plain English, are democracies of *inequality*, democracies of *gross inequality*. That is the unavoidable conclusion. They are much more unequal than the ludicrous employment laws about women and Catholics. They are much more unequal than the crazy union where some members have 100 votes each, or the university where the economists have 100 times the say of other faculty members. Our democracies are such that the top tenth of citizens, economically speaking, as a result of a collection of considerations of which you have heard, have about 1,000 times more political power than the bottom tenth.

Do you say I have just plucked that figure out of the air? Indeed I have. Where else would I get it? I sure wouldn't be able to get it from our economists and political scientists. But I got it out of the air that is also the collection of propositions of inequality of which you have heard. The political inequality in our societies is a lot closer to 1,000 to one than 100 to one. Don't forget that the bottom tenth in our societies has no money at all to spend on getting the right people elected, maybe no money to get to the polling station.

To put the conclusion another way, a little less speculative, our democracies are just *hierarchic democracies*. They are just *primitive democracies*. They are systems of government where the distribution of political power is systematically and absurdly unequal. *That* seems to me indisputable.

They are therefore systems of government exactly not true to the idea that two heads are better than one and more heads better than two. They are systems where only some heads get to speak, only some heads are heard. They are systems where there is no real spread of ideas under consideration, no true conflict of ideas, no real resistance to excessive self-interest, no real hearing of all the interests, no actual testing of assumptions and decisions by recourse to wide debate and open argument.

They are systems of governments where some of us deprive all of us of the benefit of really hearing all voices rather than one or some. They are systems of government that act without being subject to knowledge on the part of their electors, systems that are freed by the ignorance of their electors and their incapability or weakness of judgement. They are governments that are in ways ignorant and weak in judgement themselves, sometimes because they have not come to feel what they somehow know. What we have is near enough to thinking and inquiry subject to covert plutocracy. That is no intrinsically radical proposition, by the way. The liberal John Stuart Mill stated something close to it quite a while ago. Conservatives can be found who celebrate it, in fact by relying on an undemocratic or elitist argument for our democracy.

Not all of us will celebrate something else, to which we have not paid attention and which needs mentioning. Remember that the traditional conception of democracy included an idea about the procedure of democratic governments – the idea that elected governments themselves proceed by free and equal majority vote. There is some variant of this particular proposition about two heads being better than one and more heads better than two in the up-to-date conception of democracy. That democracy in any conception includes some such recommendation must certainly be part of the argument for saying that democracy gets things more right or less wrong than other systems of government.

The recommendation with respect to our existing democracies needs thinking about, to say the least. In March 2003 Britain went to war in Iraq. What needs saying about the war now, whatever is to be said later, is that the House of Commons, the very forum of this democracy, was prevented from voting on this war, a war against which hundreds of thousands of people, maybe a million, were marching in the streets. The House of Commons was constitutionally prevented from voting for fear of the outcome, maybe a very small majority for the government. It was exactly the *will* of the leader of the government that was most significant in taking Britain into the war.

I grant that there remains a lot of point in comparing our democracies favourably to dictatorships and the like. I'd rather live here, under the dim leader of a dim government. But there is at least as much point in comparing our democracies to democracies that are not hierarchic or would not be hierarchic. These are at least very important alternatives for us right now. What I mean is that these comparisons need to be in mind when we are looking, to revert to the main point, at the contribution of a society's location on an equality/inequality scale to getting things right. The comparisons need to be kept in mind when we are looking at societies with the idea that two heads are better than one and more heads better than two.

The general idea we have been considering is that our democracy gets things right or less wrong or is in the right or more in the right because of the equality in it. And that because of the equality in it, it gets things right about Palestine, 9/11, Iraq and 7/7. That is a nonsense. Anyway the premise is a nonsense.

Democracy's Freedom

Once you get started in actually thinking about democracy, it is hard to stop. Something else can come to you. It has to do with what was mentioned as the first of the three features of democracy in both the traditional and the up-to-date conceptions – the people *freely* choose governments in an election and then *freely* influence governments between elections and also the agenda for the next election, what comes up for consideration.

What we have so far is that the worth of the judgements of our democracy is at least put in doubt, surely made worthless sometimes, by the fact that it is nothing like true in our democracy that all heads count equally. Does that leave untouched something that has been distinguished from the matter of equality? That is indeed freedom. You will not need reminding that freedom by itself is made much of by our political leaders. When they are not contrasting democracy itself with terrorism as they understand it, they are contrasting our freedom in particular with terrorism.

And, to press on with our present inquiry, freedom is taken as another reason for trusting the upshots of the democratic decision-procedure.

This needs to be distinguished from something else we can grant and put aside, another and lesser recommendation of the freedom in democracy. That recommendation is the *exercise* or *experience* of political freedom. That in itself is a satisfaction – leaving aside the upshot of the exercise in terms of legislation or starting a war or whatever. Having a say is good in itself.

But the main recommendation of the political freedom in democracy, anyway the main possible recommendation, is indeed not the experience of it but exactly what we have been considering in connection with the equality, the consequences or results of the freedom, what it contributes to, the good or better judgement. So where we are in the story is that if our democracies are not to be trusted greatly more than those other governments on grounds of the equality in them, maybe they *are* to be trusted on grounds of freedom in them. The citizens in a democracy are not silenced, constrained to vote one way, compelled to go on demonstrations.

But you can think a little more about this freedom, and, as it turns out, equality again.

There used to be a conservative and maybe liberal refrain in politics and political philosophy. No doubt there still is. The refrain is that freedom, also called liberty, is inconsistent with equality. You can't have them both. Pretty clearly, then, they are two things, such that you can have one without the other, indeed such that you have to have one without the other. Whatever else we have been assuming so far in connection with democracy, we too have been assuming that equality and freedom are two things.

That turns out to be wrong – another reason, incidentally, for reflecting on the intelligence of the conventions of our societies. Equality and freedom can instead be said to be one thing in an important sense. At any rate, they rise and fall together. That is the result of a certain line of reflection.

The central facts in it are simple enough. Freedom, as we have been supposing, is deciding and acting as you want, without being compelled or constrained to decide or act in one way rather than another. Freedom is thus a matter of degree – we may be under no compulsion or constraint at all, or a little or a lot, or, as we say, be left with no choice at all. And the degree of freedom you have, to come to another point, may be dependent on the degree of freedom I have. Or, as it may sometimes be better or more natural to say, the degree of freedom you have depends on the means you have, and your amount or worth of means may depend on my amount or worth.

For example, you have a lot less freedom than me in a certain situation if I have a gun. You have a lot less freedom in some situation if you are poor and I am better off or rich. You have less political freedom than I do if I can buy a lot of television commercials to get my candidate elected. These freedoms, to come to the principal point in all this, depend on degrees of equality or inequality in them or the means to them. As equality in freedom or means to freedom decreases, so does somebody's freedom, right down to zero.

In general, freedoms may have to be something like equal, *really* something like equal, in order to be freedoms at all. Or, at any rate, any worth of freedoms depends on their really being something like equal.

So you have to ask a question about a freedom or a freedom so called before you are sold it as worth something, maybe as giving rise to good judgement in a society. You have to ask what degree of equality or inequality it involves. You have to ask about any freedom or freedom so called, before you are sold it by a salesman for democracy as a guide to right and wrong, what degree of equality or inequality it involves. This freedom and the good of it is a function of how equally it is shared. This freedom or freedom so called, like any other one, shades off into unfreedom. It shades off into constraint, impotence or oppression as the degree of equality lessens.

The conclusion to which we come is clear. Just as there is no real or strong argument for the good judgement of our democracy based on the supposed equality of it, so there is no real argument that can be based on the supposed freedom of it. We cannot really proceed by way of either an argument from equality or an argument from freedom to the conclusion that our hierarchic or primitive democracy should be our guide as to right and wrong in the world, and in particular right and wrong in Palestine, Iraq and elsewhere.

If you want to go back to the conservative and maybe liberal refrain on the supposed conflict between freedom and equality, by the way, the reality there is clear enough. It is not some general conflict between freedom and equality at all, but really some or other conflict between *one* especially chosen freedom, somehow or supposedly equal, and another somehow or supposedly equal freedom. It can be the conflict between a freedom having to do with private property or a market and a freedom having to do with health care or poverty. So, too, incidentally, was a supposed conflict between *rights* and equality just a conflict between various different rights, but let us not get into that.

Maybe a word or two is needed on something else. In my saying freedom depends on equality, do you think I am confusing freedom and power? Do you say not having freedom is indeed being compelled or constrained to do something? And that that is quite different from not having the power to do the thing? And that what equality may affect is power, not freedom?

Part of the reply to the objection is that we can talk either way – take freedom as including not being compelled and also having the power to do something, or take freedom as just being the first thing. The other part of the answer is that it doesn't actually matter to the argument we have gone through if you talk the first and more inclusive way. In this case a certain good depends on both freedom and power, and both these things are goods dependent on equality and inequality.

Another thought. What you have heard about the connections between freedom and equality is in fact truistic, or should be. What you have heard is assumed in our ordinary talk about freedom and equality, including the earlier talk in these sections of this book. Look back to the top of p. 41 and the sentence you read: 'The people are not compelled or constrained in this choosing and influencing of governments'. You understood the freedom to involve equality, didn't you? How could you fail to? What is not a matter of truism is the operation of convention in our society, the making of assent, whereby it is possible to think otherwise for a while or for ever.

One more thought. It is worth noticing in anticipation of something coming soon in our inquiry about human goods and equality that the dependency of your freedom on mine does not make our freedoms into only what are called relative rather than absolute goods. An absolute good is *some or enough or much or a lot* of something. A relative good, usually taken to be less important, is *more than* another amount of something. An absolute good, to put the point differently, is something at some point on a scale of some sort or other, not necessarily a numerical scale. A relative good, so called, is something's being to an extent higher on the scale than something else – a relationship in which various other pairs of goods up and down the scale may also stand.

It should be absolutely clear, even to Bush and Blair, that my freedom's dependence on yours does not make my freedom into only a relative good.

Democracy's Help

When you get started actually thinking about a thing, as I say, it can indeed be hard to stop.

We have so far not questioned one idea, the basic one in the line of thought we have had in mind. You can forget the problems about equality and about freedom, and there is still another problem, a prior problem. The basic idea in our line of thought is that democracy is a decision-procedure whose decisions can be known to have a great recommendation before you know what they are.

The line of thought is not that you already somehow know a decision is right or sensible or whatever, and then get reassurance from thinking it came from democracy. That would leave untouched the main question, of how you find out a decision is right or sensible or whatever in the first place. The basic idea is that you can operate democracy before you can see what is right and thereby find out. It is in a sense a blind decision procedure.

Put this way, the line of thought may be less compelling than you earlier supposed. But it is in fact what we have been considering, and an idea like it has been popular in recent moral and political philosophy of a liberal kind.

Rawls's three principles of liberalism were that our societies are first to be run according to certain traditional rights or liberties, and then according to a principle of equal opportunity, and then according to the principle that there is to be whatever inequality makes a worst-off class better off than it would be without the inequality. An argument for these principles was elaborated by him, at bottom a piece of imagination.

What was imagined was a certain decision-procedure, a making of a social contract by people setting up a society. It was maintained that the entirely exceptional situation of the persons, most notably each one's total ignorance of his or her own personal characteristics and interests, would recommend whatever they decided on by way of a society. It was concluded that these people would choose Rawls's three principles. It was thereby concluded that these principles would be right for us in the world as it is. Another blind decision procedure. Or indeed double-blind – both we and the imagined contractors are in the state.

The contract argument got a lot of philosophical attention. You could see, though, without the attention, that the imagined decision and the conclusion for us were in a way foreordained. What was actually happening was that the principles were in some form in at the beginning of the argument – in the specified situation of the imagined contractors.

For a start, they had to have a conviction about the traditional liberties. They couldn't be a bunch of left-over communists. They had to think those liberties, including a liberty of private property, more important than equality of opportunity in giving rise to a kind of society. They also had to think that equality of opportunity is more important than the condition of a worst-off class. In fact not a blind decision procedure at all. Rawls, to his credit, remarked that a contract method might not produce principles you like. In that case, he said, you could go back and change the circumstance of the imagined contractors, indeed change the contractors, to get the principles you wanted.

What about democracy then? Is it really conceivable that you can start with democracy as a method or decision-procedure, keep in mind its equality and freedom, know nothing or little about what it will produce, and get to an answer about social justice or the just society or whatever, an answer about how societies ought to run – and an answer about right and wrong to questions we are contemplating about Palestine and so on?

Of course not. You are going to understand democracy in such a way that you are as good as guaranteed to get a certain upshot or range of upshots. You're not expecting it might endorse al-Qaeda are you? After all, it's *our* democracy you are talking about, and you know a lot about how it works and what it results in. You haven't been asleep for twenty years, have you, or not reading the papers? So the supposed democracy argument will have been pretty circular, a begging of the question. You somehow start with what you presumably think is right, which is inherent in democracy, and then you conclude it is right. But you will need an actual argument for the upshot, what you took to be right in the first place, something not about democracy.

You can be asked to speak up about what you are inexplicitly feeding into the procedure in the first place. You can be asked if what you are feeding in is whatever liberalism comes to. You can be asked something else, given the known politics of the best-off tenths of population in income and wealth. You can be asked if what you are feeding in to the procedure in the first place is exactly conservatism and its rationale.

That Rawls's contract argument and the argument from democracy are essentially circular, by the way, goes together with another simple fact from well outside the world of political philosophy. It is *always* exactly a history of upshots that recommends a decision-procedure, or a history of upshots of similar or related decision-procedures. Nothing else could. This is the case, for example, with courts of law, despite unpredictability with particular cases. It is the case in all of life, starting with the rule that the child who cuts the cake gets the last slice. It is anticipated upshots of a general kind that recommend a new decision-procedure. Nothing else could.

Does any more need to be said about democracy's supposed help in getting us to the moral truth about our subjects? No doubt the idea that it does had to be considered. But in fact, if you will put up with some plain speaking, the idea is hardly worth grown-up attention. It falls down when you think about any of equality, freedom, or the basic idea of the decision-procedure.

It would have been simpler to pass right by the matter of the nature of democracy, its description, and just ask about its consequences in the world as we have it, its contribution to famine, war and the like. Do they recommend it anything like consistently? It comes to mind again that democracy used to be argued for as the system of government that reduces the probability of war. Well, tell that to the marines in Iraq. Tell it to the Iraqis. Tell it to the dead ones.

We could have spent some time too on a complication. That is the fact that some terrorism, including Palestinian terrorism, actually has the goal of nothing other than democracy. It is aimed at getting democratic self-government in a homeland. There is reason to call it democratic terrorism, of which you may hear a little more.

We could have noted a little earlier, too, that there is a big difference between telling somebody to trust some method for getting to a principle of right and wrong and instead actually laying out the principle you think it produces. I don't mean laying out what you put in at the beginning, which might take some speculation and self-inquiry, but something simpler – laying out what we get out, in fact what we have got out already. After all, this democracy has been running for quite a while. It's not as if we're about to turn it on. There was everything to be said for a direct report on the product – conservatism or liberalism as you understand it or whatever else. You could have just told us, couldn't you? You could have explained, I guess, how it is that our democratic governments have made more contribution than any other governments to a loss of twenty million years of living time by a sample of Africans now still alive?

There is everything to be said for some different directness right now.

The Principle of Humanity

There is a morality to which we are all committed, by two things. The first is the great goods of our lives, the objects of our great desires – which great goods issue in each of us making and being certain of moral judgements about our having them ourselves. The other thing is our minimal rationality, just the fact of our having reasons, including moral reasons, necessarily as general as any other reasons. In short, we are committed to a morality of good consequences by our human nature.

We all desire the great good of going on existing, where that does not mean a lot more than just being conscious, being in the world. As you can also say, to the same effect, we want a personal world to go on longer. We have the same desire for those close to us, our children first. This desire can sometimes be defeated by others. It comes to mind that a lot of American men and women would have ended their own worlds, carried out suicide missions, to prevent the 2,800 deaths on 9/11. Nonetheless, despite exceptions, this existence is something almost all of us crave. We crave *a decent length of life*. Say 75 years rather than 35.

A second desire we all have is for a quality of life in a certain sense. This is a kind of existence that has a lot to do with our bodies. We want not to be in pain, to have satisfactions of food, drink, shelter, safety, sleep, maybe sex. As that implies, and as is also the case with the first desire, we also want the material means to the end in question, the material means to this *bodily quality of life*. Some of the means are some of the consumer-goods, so called, easier to be superior about if you have them. You are likely to lack these means if you are in poverty.

A third thing we all want is *freedom and power*. We do not want to be coerced by personal circumstances arranged by others, bullied, subjected to compulsion, unable to run our own lives, weakened. We want this voluntariness and strength in a range of settings, from a house, neighbourhood and place of work to the greatest and maybe most important setting, a society in a homeland. It is no oddity that freedom from something is what is promised by *every* political or national tradition or movement without exception – and secured to some extent if it is in control.

Another of our shared desires is for goods of *relationship* to those around us. We want kinds of connections with these other people. Each of us wants the unique loyalty and if possible the love of one other person, maybe two or three. We also want to be members of larger groups. No one wants to be cut off by his or her own feelings from the surrounding society or cut off from it by others' feelings. This was a considerable part of why it was no good being a *nigger* or a *Jew* or a *Paki* in places where those words were spoken as they were.

A fifth desire, not far away from the one for relationship, is for *respect and self-respect*. No one wants to feel worthless. No one is untouched by disdain, even stupid disdain. No one wants humiliation. Persons kill themselves, and others, because of it. We do not want humiliation for our people either. As in the case of all these great desires, this one for respect and self-respect extends to others close to us, and in ways to other people, and it goes with desires for the means to the ends.

Finally, we want the *goods of culture*. All of us want at least some of them. Many of us want the practice and reassurance of a religion, or the custom of a people, or indeed a kind of society. We may want not to live in what we take to be a degraded society, maybe one that gives an ascendancy to buying and selling in its social policies and has a public preoccupation with sex. All of us with a glimmer of knowledge want the good of knowledge and thus of education. All with a glimmer of what is written down want to be able to read. We also want diversion if not art.

These, by one way of counting them, are our fundamental desires for the great goods. Certainly they are interrelated goods. If the first is necessary to all the others, and several are in other relations of necessity, there is no great point in trying to rank them. You may if you want speak of these fundamental desires as needs. But the usage obscures a little the plain fact of them. The desires are a premise of fact for other things, a premise in which no disputable moral standard has a part, or such an uncertain idea as what is called flourishing, the result of having needs satisfied.

A *bad life*, we take it, is to be defined in terms of the deprivation of some or all of these goods, the frustration of some or all of these desires. A *good life* is defined in terms of satisfaction of them. There is a need for decision here as to bad lives and good lives, as well as the registering of facts. That is what you would expect in the formulation or stating of a moral principle, which is what we are now engaged in. A bad life, we will take it, quickly here, is one that lacks one or more of the first three goods – subsistence, a bodily quality of life, all freedom and power – or a life of subsistence that is only minimally satisfied with respect to the other five goods. Good lives are had by all other persons.

The Principle of Humanity has to do with bad lives. It is not well expressed, indeed not expressed at all, as the truistic principle that we should rescue those with bad lives, those who are badly off. It is the principle that *we must actually take rational steps to the end of getting and keeping people out of bad lives.*

That is, we should take steps that are rational in the ordinary sense of actually having a good probability of securing the consequence. These are not steps that are pieces of self-deception, pretence or speechifying, but steps that you can actually reasonably believe will be effective, will serve the end. In being rational in the ordinary way, of course, they will also be something else in addition to being effective, quite as important. They will have to be well judged, sensible or economical in terms of well-being, not be likely to cause more distress than they prevent, not be self-defeating in that way.

The Principle of Humanity, to state it a bit more fully, is that *the right or justified thing as distinct from others – the right action, practice, institution, government, society or possible world – is the one that according to the best judgement and information is the rational one in the sense of being effective and not self-defeating with respect to the end of getting and keeping people out of bad lives.*

The principle covers positive acts or commissions and the like – detonating the bomb, firing the missile from the helicopter gunship, financing ethnic cleansing, taking over the airliner, hunting killers, starting a war, lying about it, fighting back against occupiers, blowing up yourself and the people in the subway train, guarding the city against more attacks. The principle also covers those other actions that are omissions – not stopping the bomber you can stop, not stopping the helicopter pilot, not doing what could be done to make a world not so unjust or vicious that it provides a context for such horrific acts as the flying of airliners into towers, not being vigilant, not doing what would make war less likely, not trying to improve your democracy, not calling the police or saying something about racism.

That is to say that the principle is about actions or conduct in general and the things into which they enter. It is about our behaviour that is intentional in some way and degree. Acts and omissions, which shade into one another rather than fall into two categories, are distinguished by their intentions. Acts are likely to be fully intentional – they are behaviour whose natures and consequences are represented and desired in the intentions of the agents. What we call omissions, in contrast, may be actions that are partly intentional – actions whose natures and consequences are not pictured and desired by the person acting, but as a result of earlier intentions and actions of the person.

For example, I do not contribute to a famine charity by using the money in another way, going on a holiday. What the omission comes to is not attending to the action in its nature and consequences as an omission, not attending as a result of earlier intentions and actions. For another example, a leader or an electorate does something that is also failing to stop genocide because the leader or the electorate have earlier done something like resolve to give their awareness to other things.

There are also unintentional omissions. Here the fact that the nature and effects of an action are not in the agent's intention is not the result of his or her earlier activity. They are of importance, and should claim attention. But we do not need to dwell on them now.

There have been attempts to find a difference of fact between acts and omissions such that there is a general difference between them in terms of rightness and wrongness. The attempts have never come near to succeeding. There have been attempts to show that any act whose probable consequences are identical with those of an omission can be wrong while the omission is right. No attempt has succeeded.

The most important attempt, having to do with intentions, fails for the reason accepted in ways by all of us, that what makes actions right is not intentions of agents. It is clear indeed that two actions can both be wrong, one of which is done out of the best of intentions and the other the worst. The simplest case is where the best intention is conjoined with a terrible but not a culpable mistake in belief. Very commonly, as well, people do the right thing out of a low intention. That I get no moral credit at all for the action does not make the action wrong. Nor does integrity or character help any more than intentions with right actions. Hitler's actions would not become more right by way of an absolute proof of his integrity, his having remained true to his deepest principle.

The Principle of Humanity does give an importance to intentions, however, and to the moral responsibility of people for their actions, and to the standing or decency or humanity of people over time. It gives these things importance in relation to what is fundamentally important – securing the right action, practice, institution, foreign policy, contribution to a kind of world. And with these actions and the like, to repeat, it does not make any general difference in rightness between acts and at least partly intentional omissions.

The principle is not unusual in this. Who thinks, or who says when they are thinking, that it is all right for you to let someone or half of a people starve to death if you have arranged to have your mind on something else? Who thinks it is all right to carry on your life, maybe your political life, while the large-eyed children in those photographs fade away into their deaths? If conservative philosophers of property can be found to excuse and justify us, morality and moral philosophy in general are in this respect not so brazen in their exonerations as they used to be.

There is a somewhat related and smaller matter that needs to be noticed here. You will of course have understood that the Principle of Humanity is to the effect that we are to consider *all* the foreseeable consequences of an action in terms of bad lives. To act on the idea of considering only bad lives of Muslims, or bad lives of Jews, or of any other group, would be to go against the principle absolutely. It is the preventing of bad lives that is fundamental. Relatedly, there will be no possibility at all of saying that firing a missile or setting a bomb is to be considered only in terms of deaths that are in some sense or other intended, as distinct from other deaths foreseen but in some sense not intended, deaths of innocents somehow understood. This matter, which arises with more moralities than that of the Principle of Humanity, is one we will be coming back to.

To leave the attitude of the Principle of Humanity to acts and omissions, another large truth about it is its end or goal. If it is the fundamental principle of justice or decency, its end or goal is not equality. It is not the end of getting everybody on a level, let alone making everybody the same. The end is not a relational one at all, not what has been objected to in egalitarianism. It is not open to the question, 'What is so good about making people equal if they could all be unequally better off?' The end, as stated, is the end of saving people from bad lives. It would demand urgent action, exactly as urgent, in a world where everyone had perfectly equal lives, all equally bad. So it is a principle of humanity, fellow-feeling or generosity rather than of equality – despite the great importance of *certain* equalities, notably in freedoms. These equalities are greatly important as means to the end of the principle.

The Principle of Humanity is indeed fundamental to the morality of humanity. It is a summary of a kind that is necessary to any morality. It is its basis and rationale. That is not to say that it is anything like the complete morality in itself. A further and necessary understanding of the morality of humanity is to be had first by way of a number of policies and practices that give further content to the principle, and then by way of an account of its character.

The first policy is to transfer certain means to well-being, material and also other means, from the better off to the badly off. These are means whose transfer would in fact not significantly affect the well-being of the better off. An immense amount of these means exist. They are now wasted. Remember what we throw out, and, more importantly, what our businesses and corporations discard, leave to decay or ruin. Think about the industry of packaging things, of the costs in commercial competition that are of no benefit at all to most of us.

The second policy is means-transfer that *would* reduce the well-being of the better-off, but without increasing the number of bad lives. The people from whom the means would be taken would still have good lives. An immense amount of these means exist. As in the case of the first policy, some consist in land, and land of a people. For this reason among others, what you are hearing about is not Rawls's theory of justice or a variant of it.

The third policy, of great importance, is about material incentive-rewards. It would reduce them to those that are *actually necessary*, and actually necessary in terms of the goal of the Principle of Humanity. They will not be the rewards now demanded. They will not be the incentive-rewards that issue in the best-off tenth of Americans having 30 per cent of the income and 70 per cent of the wealth while the bottom tenth has 2 per cent and none. They will not be the rewards called for by the most absurd of propositions in our lives, that the rich have to be just as rich as they are in order for the wretched not to be more wretched. They will not be the rewards and lack of them suddenly visible to all in New Orleans after the hurricane in 2005.

You will naturally take these three policies to exclude something else. But this exclusion had better be stated explicitly as a fourth policy. It is that in general, means to well-being are not to be redirected to the well off unnecessarily, as supposed incentives or as anything else, say proper taxation policies, so as to improve their already satisfied lives. This fattening is excluded.

The fifth policy, also implicit in the others, is against violence and near-violence. Therefore it is against terrorism and war. But like all such policies rightly called realistic, it cannot be an absolute or completely general prohibition. Like all of them, it accommodates some possibility of justified war. Like fewer alternative policies, including one to be taken from the UN Declaration of Rights, it can contemplate the possibility of justified action that falls under the name of terrorism. If it may give some limited role to a distinction between official and non-official killing, it does not immediately exclude some things mentioned earlier, including violence by victims whose oppressors leave them no other option and then sanctimoniously condemn the violence. Also, the policy sees the need for police forces, some punishment by the state, some self-defence, and so on.

A further understanding of the Principle of Humanity, as necessary, comes from what can be distinguished from policies, which is practices.

You have heard that the end or goal of the principle is getting people out of bad lives, not getting them into equal lives – whatever large side-effects of equality there may be of progress towards the end or goal. The end is not at all open to the objection to egalitarianism that it does not matter in itself if someone has more or less or the same as someone else, but how much they have. But the end of humanity is consistent with something else. It is that we are to use the means of certain practices of equality to get people out of bad lives. Practices of equality are not the only but they are the most important of the practices serving the end of saving men, women and children from deprivation, distress and wretchedness.

A main point here was in view in connection with the argument for a good democracy. The first way to secure the moral rights of those with bad lives is to give them equal voices. Another way is for them to claim their moral rights by themselves making their voices heard. What they must have is the same hearing as the rest of us, or rather some of the rest of us. Any practice of equality that serves that intermediate or instrumental goal, an advance in democracy, must be something that serves humanity.

There are other practices of equality as important. One is a true equality of opportunity. It will certainly include special opportunity for those who have been deprived of the means of developing and displaying their abilities. Other practices have to do with the fact of our common membership of a species. We must, despite all differences between us, have common needs. That fact brings with it a truth to the effect that to seek to make bad lives good must be to proceed on the basis of an assumption of equality about, first of all, food.

To which needs to be added a large proposition that no doubt you will remember. Freedom, a great part of a good life, is one with equality, or at least dependent on it. How much you have of freedom depends on how much I have. The means to freedom is equalities. That does not make equality, a relative good, the end of a struggle for freedom. It leaves freedom as the end of the struggle, something that is a place on a scale, a fact of voluntariness or non-compulsion, not itself a relationship to other places on the scale.

All of this statement of the Principle of Humanity, anyway most of it, might suggest that it is a principle for one large side of life but not a complete principle. You might get the idea from its focus and concentration, and in particular the public policies, that it does not cover private life, or relations between people all of whom have good lives, or relations between men and women, or matters of religion, or contracts between individuals, and the like. That is not true, for several reasons.

For a start, there are bad lives in all sides or parts of our existence. Further, if you suppose that a morality needs to have in it particular sections concerned with private life, relations between people with good lives and so on – rules or ideals or whatever having to do with these – that does not go against the Principle of Humanity. What it requires is that whatever is said and done about these things is to be consistent with the principle itself, serve its end.

The Character of the Principle

There is something as important to the morality of humanity as what we have – the principle about bad lives that summarizes it, its view of omissions, its policies and its practices. There is what can be called the character or nature of the principle and the morality. That character or nature, as with other principles and moralities, has a good deal in it.

It is not unreflective about morality or about itself. It is, to speak plainly, not ignorant, naïve, simple, self-serving or political about the nature of all moral principles, judgements and the like. It is saved from unreflectiveness by knowing a little philosophy.

If it sees that a decent moral principle is rightly called that, exactly a decent moral principle, and that some such thing is as important as truth itself, it also sees any such principle is an *attitude* – an attitude capable of being supported by facts and by a general logic. It takes any attitude whatever to be a valuing of something and hence to involve desire, which valuing may or may not conceive of the thing clearly and entirely.

Thus the Principle of Humanity does not begin to suppose that alternative or competing moralities and politics, of any kind, can be different or have any other standing or be in less need of the support of facts and logic. It does not at all contemplate that it faces alternatives or competitors that have any sort of higher or deeper authority, certification or imprimatur. It does not half-respect the ordinary stuff of most politicians, their self-defensive argot for a time, maybe that this or that is *unacceptable*. In general the principle does not pretend a piety about morality that no one who is reflective can sustain.

Morality is not something given by God, or ancient texts, or any religion high or low. It is not given to persons of special perception and sensitivity of whatever kind. Nor is morality something given to a social class or a tradition of one people, or proved by their special success, least of all their material success or vulgarity. It is not owed to any other special fact about a people, such as their power or weakness. As you have heard, morality is not the property of a political tradition or inclination, or of a commitment to democracy, let alone democratic politicians.

Do you recall my remarking in connection with the politics of reality that there have long been denigrating utterances about morality as consisting in mere value judgements, subjectivity, emotive meaning and the like? There is a distinction between all that and what has just been said. It is that morality is no more than and no less than attitudes capable of being supported by facts and logic.

A second point about the Principle of Humanity is that it is in a way a literal one. It is not the sort of thing uttered in much the same words by the estimable Bill Clinton, as indeed it was, or conceivably by Brown of the New Labour Party, he of whom some have hopes despite the fact that he has not yet by any public action distinguished himself from his leader Blair. You can say the principle is a different speech-act than theirs.

It does imply, for a start, that we are to hold our leaders and those around them morally responsible when they violate it in the way that we have feeling against lesser wrongdoers in our jails. The principle does not presuppose a difference in kind in this respect, whatever else can be said, between a prime minister and a pornographer, or a prime minister and a child-molester, rapist or murderer.

Nor is the principle meant to be an exhortation already understood as not likely to be acted on in fact, let alone understood as something that cannot be acted on in fact. We are actually to do what is actually rational to get and keep people out of bad lives, not engage in substitute behaviour, maybe giving undertakings to estimable rock stars arranging concerts about African poverty, just in time for the world's richest nations to meet again and do nothing much about it.

The principle, as you will have taken in, is not that of conservatism or liberalism. Something close to the principle or very like it has been the source and inspiration of the UN Declaration of Human Rights, many UN resolutions, and a clear and essential part of the rest of international law. Also, I think, the doctrine of the just war. The principle has indeed been the guide or ideal of the Left in politics so long as the Left has been true to itself.

That is not to say, you will gather, that it sanctions all the theory, commitments, practices and other means of all the traditions, parties and persons within the history or the present of the Left in politics. The principle is itself and not another thing. Its explanation depends on no other ideology. It is not vulnerable to objections owed to mistakes made about it or in trying to act on it. It would be absurd to suppose it is so much as touched by the fact that a Wall fell down as an empire ended.

The principle, as you will also have taken in, has the fourth distinction of not operating with a merely generic notion, say happiness, well-being, deprivation, justice, fairness or the like, let alone the common good or community. It is not theoretical in a way that lets the world slip out of view or out of focus.

So it is not like utilitarianism or some morality of economists, which by going on about general happiness or satisfaction or whatever makes it more possible, even with good will, to slide by individual costs of a general happiness, to overlook victimization if not actually justify it. Rather, the Principle of Humanity fixes attention on realities that do not so easily allow us to overlook the lives of others, rise above or disregard them. It is in its character closer to life, closer to other lives than our own.

The principle is also clear. It does not have the hopeless indeterminacy of Kant's celebrated injunction that was also called the Principle of Humanity. That was the injunction that we are to treat each person as an end and not only as a means. It can be understood to mean almost anything, down to a mild piece of advice to respect everyone, a piece of advice consistent with leaving them in misery. Nor does our principle have what is effectively the vapidity of 'Love your neighbour', however related it may be in spirit. It has more in it than the well-meant help of the Archbishop of Canterbury.

The Principle of Humanity, sixthly, to come on to something still larger, is a principle of truth, in several ways. In fact, a commitment to truth is just about the bottom of it.

As you will anticipate, it is not respectful of any orthodoxies of opinion and reaction that have been put in place or at any rate come to be in place, many about supposed facts, in particular supposed necessities. It does not always call terrorism something else, such as resistance, thereby tending to leave out the killing and maiming. Nor does it fail to see that terrorism can also *be* something else, say resistance to ethnic cleansing. It does not leave out half the facts in looking at any matter. It does not look at things from your local point of view. It disdains the denials, evasions and forgettings of truth that go with taking only some lives really to matter. It is the very contradiction of what it regards as the viciousness of what certainly is no mere statement of a right of self-preservation, the declaration on behalf of a people that 'our lives comes first'.

The principle is not deferential to any of the kinds of our societies' convention. If its commitment to reflection and argument, and of course to rationality, and in particular to argued endorsements, stands in the way of engaging in direct or indirect incitement, it is not deferential to the fact that some answers to questions have been proscribed as terrible. It is not respectful of the powers that be, including the democratic powers, but cynical at least about their self-deception. It does not accept a politician's edict with respect to certain moral judgements, say about killing, sometimes to the effect that we are all to eschew them, sometimes to the effect that we leave to the politician a monopoly on engaging in them, however evasively. It is prepared to think about atrocities, if not on the day 9/11 or the day 7/7, then sometime after. If not on a day in the refugee camps of Sabra or Shatila, or on a day in Baghdad, then sometime after.

The principle, as you will expect, is for public inquiry that issues in relevant truth, for public conduct of public business that issues in relevant truth. The principle is an attitude antithetical to the inanely resolute one of the Blair government on television in 2006 and before then. That is the attitude, in opposition to the whole history of intelligence, that the response to a question is a speech of diversion.

The principle, less importantly, can tell the difference between proper philosophical civility and sucking-up. Also the difference between considering other views and pretending that all of them are worth respect. It asserts that Nozick's picture of the perfectly just society is to be thought about with contempt.

Does the principle not only engage in and recommend truth but also rest on a foundation of it?

The Strength of the Principle

Life would be easier if morality were simpler. But the conclusions to which we are already well on the way, about the horrors of Palestine, 9/11, Iraq and 7/7 and the rest, and the light thrown on the later by the earlier events, will not depend just on the foundation of the Principle of Humanity as stated. In fact there are things that are clearer and stronger than any general principle, necessary though a general principle may be. That a man's torturing a child for the purpose of sexual excitement is monstrous in its wrong is evidently a kind of truth, somehow as strong as a plain truth of fact. It is more the case that the Principle of Humanity depends on such a moral truth than that the moral truth depends on the principle.

The morality of humanity, like any morality, has as its content and recommendation the sum of the propositions in it including its principle, and also its nature or character. Its policies and practices are part of its content. So too are the specified consequences of the principle, some being consequences that are only such in a formal sense, and stand on their own as moral truths.

Some consequences, whether or not they have that strength, are about terrorism and war. Another is the wrong of our hierarchic democracy. It is not only dim, but also a violation of the Principle of Humanity in its inequality and unfreedom, and yet more so in its products, the human facts owed to or recorded by the distributions of wealth and income. There is also the moral responsibility of its beneficiaries, those who propose to maintain it in perpetuity. You learn more of the morality of humanity by learning of such consequences. Its content is to some considerable extent given by them.

Still, for all of that, it is the Principle of Humanity that sums up the rest and offers the possibility of consistency among all certainties and judgements in the morality. Such a general principle, as you have heard, is essential. It is essential for other cases than those of absolute certainty, which is to say most cases.

Is there a general argument for the Principle of Humanity? Could there be what can have the name of being a proof, as has sometimes seemed to me possible? You heard at the start that we are all somehow committed to the Principle of Humanity. There is an argument from our human nature. It has to do with our fundamental desires, our desires for the great goods, and also with our being rational in the minimal sense of our having reasons for things, sometimes moral reasons.

Fundamentally it is an argument from consistency resting on strong premises. It cannot actually stop people from being inconsistent. No argument for anything, however good, can in itself be anything like a necessitating cause. But there is a price to be paid for inconsistency that few want and are able to pay. It is that if you say something is right, and then you also somehow say a thing of that same kind is wrong, you say nothing. A contradiction asserts nothing, gives no reason whatever for anything. And a reason is what you want to have, what you are claiming to have. That is true of all of us.

The argument from consistency for the Principle of Humanity has a number of premises in it. They can be put in terms of certain situations of choice.

Your human nature is such, you will agree, that if there is a choice between (1) your being got out of a bad life into a good one, and (2) somebody else having a good life made still better, you want the first thing to be done. Further, you give the reason that this is right. It is right that your being helped out of deprivation, misery or agony comes ahead of someone else's still fuller satisfaction in the great goods of life. This reason for having help for yourself is of its nature general. All reasons are. From your conviction about yourself, your rightful claim, arguably you are on the way to the Principle of Humanity, or at least faced in that direction.

By way of a fast example, you believe it is wrong for you to be slowly starved for a month, put in danger of your life, in order that I have my own car rather than have to go on getting to work by bus. Let alone that you be starved in order for my family to have two cars. By way of another example, you believe it would be wrong for you to be sexually degraded by Americans in a prison in Baghdad if what is gained is just my adding to the satisfactions of my good life in Washington.

Your reason for what you desire, not to be starved or put on a leash naked, because of that reason's general character, commits you to other propositions about other people with respect to additions to bad lives and good lives. That there is room for argument here does not much affect things.

But, it may be said, there is a difficulty. Something else is also true. If there is a choice between *your* already good life being improved, and somebody else being got out of a bad life, maybe nearly a good one, you may want the first, and argue that there is some moral reason for this. You may talk of desert, or family lineage, or race, or ethnic group, or democracy, or even a piece of ancient history. You will be very far from alone.

You can be faced with an objection. It will be to the effect that in what are argued to be relevantly identical situations, but where you happen to be in the bad position rather than the good one, you would judge differently. That is, you can be reminded of the first choice situation. But it will not be easy for the objector or you to succeed in this dispute, which will become one about whether the two situations are relevantly identical or close enough. Let us leave this difficulty unresolved and consider some other situations.

Suppose you contemplate two other people to whom you are not at all connected in terms of particular sympathy or degree of identification. If your choice is between an escape from a bad life for one, and an improvement of an already good life for the other, you will want the first to happen and take it to be right. That will be your tendency despite ideas of desert or whatever. Few of us talk about private property in connection with the children with the large eyes.

Consider a third situation. If your choice is between possibilities having to do only with yourself, a possibility where you escape from a bad life and a possibility where your already good life is improved, you will opt for and justify the first. If there are some exceptions to this policy of what is called maximinning, exceptions having to do with the attraction of taking a chance or gambling, they can surely be set aside as not of great consequence. Think of a choice between escaping river blindness and getting a faster car.

It is not perfectly clear how to use these situations in order to try to construct an argument for the Principle of Humanity. There is no neat proof. The argument will be to the effect that our natures are such that we give *a* precedence, if not a complete one, to reducing bad lives rather than improving good ones. The argument will not make the principle into an ordinary truth entailed by premises shown to be ordinarily true. But the argument may establish the principle as what is most consistent with judgements about ourselves that are, so to speak, the stuff of our humanity. They are real foundations, premises of ordinary truth. No other principle of morality, you can think, has such foundations.

Are they enough to allow us to speak of the principle's moral truth? How good does a general argument for a principle have to be? That is not obvious. It does seem that these considerations of our human nature do better to support the Principle of Humanity than any other considerations, of human nature or anything else, support any other principle.

There is one more thing. We all do accept the Principle of Humanity in another way, one that is less theoretical and perhaps is more telling. We accept it in actual lived disputes as distinct from reflection about imagined disputes. If you are engaged in real-life argument with somebody about right and wrong with respect to large questions, and you announce yourself as proceeding from or basing yourself on something like the Principle of Humanity, you are very likely indeed to hear from the other side, at any rate in the end, that the very same is true of it.

What neo-Zionist who is a serious adversary in argument depends on an ancient piece of religion about a people chosen by God? Or a proposition about an ancient Jewish kingdom easily met by other historical propositions? What neo-Zionist who is a serious adversary, in order to establish a right centuries later to disperse further another people and do worse than that, claims that right on the basis of a divine ordinance accepted by no one else, or half of a declaration by the British Foreign Secretary Balfour, or because of a fact of democracy? Does he say that it is because somebody paid money to an absentee landlord in Paris that a peasant family is driven out and has to die in a refugee camp?

You will hear from such an adversary, rather, about many lives of his own people taken in the recent past, about danger and safety now, about freedom, respect and being unhumiliated, about his people being together, their having their culture. You will hear about things that matter.

So with those who defend Islamic terrorism, and those who justify the war in Iraq. They show by their recourse to argument from the great human goods that other considerations, say international law or religion or whatever in themselves, are not taken by them to be true foundations of argument. With the war in Iraq and international law, does Blair serve as a stark example? Having started with the justification of international law, he got around to justification of humanitarianism.

The Principle of Humanity is not itself a general truth of fact. Like all other such things, it is an attitude, as you have heard. But it is a unique one. It would indeed be entirely misleading to dismiss it as just another value judgement, subjective, a matter of relativity in morals, or emotive meaning.

The Ends and the Means Justify the Means

A grand division used to be made or anyway attempted among various moralities and moral philosophies. Sometimes it still is. Deontological moralities and moral philosophies are said to assert duties, obligations and principles that do not have anything to do with the foreseeable consequences or results of actions. They have to do with values entirely different from the great human goods and lesser such goods.

The clearest of these may be duties or more likely rights that are said to exist just on account of our relationships to others, say our children. Other principles may seem to make sense in asserting that good intentions, maybe the pure good will, or integrity, or moral intuition, or a hold on the virtues, are fundamental to how we ought to live our lives. Or we may hear of the value of justice, where that has to do with the law rather than the good of the law, or rights, where those are taken seriously without being given a basis that explains why by recourse to something like the Principle of Humanity.

Immanuel Kant, the German philosopher, asserted that the pure good will is the only thing that matters. Also that promises should be kept despite bad effects of doing so, even catastrophic effects. He asserted too that all criminals are to be punished to the full extent of the law even if, as would ordinarily be said, no good whatever comes of this. Desert or retribution, and not anything like the prevention of offences, is the only justification of punishment in a society. If an island people decide to bring their society to an end, scatter themselves through the whole world, so that they no longer have any social purpose at all, it is their obligation to execute the last murderer in prison before getting into the boats.

In contrast with all this, we hear, are what used to be called teleological and now are called consequentialist moralities and moral philosophies. They assert principles, duties and so on that do have to do with foreseeable good results. The theories that try to justify punishment by its prevention of offences are plain examples. The English moral philosophy of utilitarianism, disaster though it was, is a large example. It still influences a certain amount of political, bureaucratic and like thinking.

For several reasons the division between the two things has become at least uncertain. One plain reason is that deontological moralities were dragged into the twentieth century. They had to admit that it cannot be right simply to *ignore* the coming bad or appalling effects of actions in considering whether they are right or wrong. So promises can sometimes be broken, and punishment has to do *some* good as well as be deserved in order to be justified. But to my mind, the deontological parts of the updated moralities do not fare at all well. Let us consider the matter.

What is it to give as a reason, for the rightness of someone's getting or having something, that he *deserves* it? No satisfactory answer, necessarily an answer that does not beg the question by understanding a deserved thing to be right by definition, has ever been given. As for reasons for doing a thing because of your relation to someone else or others, your child or your people, it is perfectly possible to accommodate these to a considerable extent in the moralities concerned with good effects. And, as can certainly be argued, to go beyond this extent of accommodation is not to do something that can be defended morally.

That is, the morality of humanity allows and enjoins me to look after my children in particular, partly by way of its practice of equality. But it does not allow me to make them fatter while other children starve. A deontological morality may say in effect that I *can* make them fatter while other children starve. It may do so by way of the intoned or declarative reason 'They are my children.' What can that be but a selfishness? Is it made less so by feeling or pompousness?

It is possible to suspect, as indeed I do, that all deontological morality is in fact lower stuff, dishonourable stuff, an abandoning of humanity, of the decent part of our nature, and an attempt to make that abandoning respectable to oneself and others. It is possible to think that what all of us are moved by is the great goods and the means to them, and related lesser goods, and that these give us our only reasons for actions, moral and other reasons. So when a deontological morality purports to give some entirely different reason for action, something else is going on under the words.

If, with punishment by the state, no worthwhile analysis can be given of the reason 'It is right to punish him because he deserves it', who can escape a certain thought? It is that what is going on is punishing in order to give satisfaction to ourselves, satisfaction in the distress of another.

As for promise-keeping, Kant's supposed proof that all promise-breaking is self-contradictory and that promise-keeping has nothing to do with good effects has convinced no one. And who would choose a world full of good intentions but also full of agony, distress and other deprivation against a world of bad intentions where things nevertheless work out very well in terms of the great goods? It would be just mad to do so, wouldn't it?

The morality of humanity is indeed a consequentialist morality.

It does indeed judge the rightness of things by certain anticipated consequences. It judges the rightness of actions, policies, practices, societies and possible worlds by certain anticipated consequences of those things, and, as it may be worth adding, *in* those things. What makes a thing worthwhile may be the doing of it, where that is of course not the intention with which it is done, or just its being in accordance with a duty or principle or relationship, but the great good of doing it – where real good is understood as the sort of thing exemplified by the great goods of the Principle of Humanity.

You have heard some objection to what is opposed to consequentialism, deontology. It is a good idea, too, to spend some time on what is said against consequentialism. It has been supposed to be at least suspect, not the kind of thing to be tolerated in higher philosophical, ethical or religious company. There are books that report on its rejection, supposedly by a significant number of moral philosophers. There are several familiar lines of resistance to particular consequentialisms, or, more likely, consequentialisms in general, bundled together and not distinguished.

The most common line of resistance is in the utterance that consequentialism as understood *takes the end to justify the means*. In one way this is plainly true. Any consequentialism takes some end to make some price paid for it worthwhile. A satisfaction or achievement makes a cost, dissatisfaction or pain worth putting up with or enduring. But what is the objection to this? The common line of resistance sounds as if there is some quite general objection to consequentialism. It has to be to that effect. Is there?

There just can't be a general objection to consequentialism since innumerable cases of it are accepted by everybody all the time. Going to the dentist is the usual example. Others are using forceful action to stop a man lying on the ground from being kicked in the head, or saying something rough and tough to stop some bullying of a child. Or having a police force. It cannot be that there is a *general* objection to all consequentialism.

The consequentialism of the Principle of Humanity, as hardly needs to be made more explicit, is in fact *not* safely expressed as being that the end justifies the means. Rather, it is that *the ends and the means justify the means*. You have heard enough about the necessity of having means that are not self-defeating, not themselves useless makers of bad lives. That was in there from the start.

An objector to any decent consequentialism must then have in mind that some *particular* end does not justify some *particular* means, or some particular group of means. He will have to show this particular want of justification, provide an argument. As the thinking and conduct of everybody shows, he cannot take his proposition to follow from some general truth. There is no such thing.

Does the objector perhaps suppose instead that some means are so terrible that *no* possible end could justify them? Well, he will have to show that. He may well be right. But he will face the difficulty that whatever he takes to be unthinkable about a means, say torture, may be avoided to a greater extent in the end in question than in any other end. In any case, he has no general argument against consequentialism.

There is also a greater difficulty for him if he is indeed questioning consequentialism in general. In any particular case he only has the hope of an objection to that particular consequentialism – and out of that objection a different consequentialism is certain to emerge. If he objects to slavery as a contemplated means to an end, he will hear in a minute about a consequentialism that excludes as wrong any actions and policies whose means include those of slavery. It will exclude the slavery, of course, on consequentialist grounds.

Another objection or resistance to consequentialism is that it does not really ask what is right, engage in proper moral thinking. Rather, as some say, it turns to *calculating what can be gained* by doing something. It looks to profit and loss. It engages in cost–benefit analysis or social engineering or collateral damage discounting or whatever.

A consequentialist can best ask what these pieces of jargon come to, what objection they are supposed to contain. Or he can make a jibe in reply, perhaps that his opponent does not look at human facts, but allows himself to be distracted. Maybe distracted by the past, as in talk of desert, or ties of relationship, as in the case of a certain extent of loyalty to one's own child or one's own people. The consequentialist can insist that he never turns away from the question of what is right, *the* moral question, but answers it in what is the human way. Clearly this kind of exchange of jibes settles nothing.

You can suppose that something lies behind or in the jibe that consequentialism does not ask what is right but calculates what can be gained. One thing is the idea that all consequentialism is or anyway is something like something already mentioned, utilitarianism. That was and remains a disaster, despite a clarity and an estimable human feeling in it.

The principle of utilitarianism or greatest happiness principle is roughly that the right thing is what is likely to produce the greatest total or maximum of satisfaction taking into account everybody affected – usually the greatest balance of satisfaction over dissatisfaction. This it may do and be committed to doing, as is well known, in an intolerable way, an unfair or unjust way, perhaps by itself making or producing bad lives. What is called punishing the innocent is one way of doing so. In recent philosophical jargon, what we need to do instead is protect certain rights, put what are called side-constraints on the aim of maximizing satisfaction. More plainly, we cannot have as our end the mere maximization of satisfaction.

This response to consequentialism, confusing it with utilitarianism, is baffling at best. Consequentialism as we have been understanding it, and presumably as it is usually understood, is not utilitarianism. As you heard, consequentialism is taken to be judging the rightness of actions and the like by probable consequences. Consequentialism is the genus or family of which utilitarianism is a species. Nor are many of the other species close to or like utilitarianism. Almost all are against it.

Certainly the Principle of Humanity is against it. In any situation, the Principle of Humanity asks the following question of fact, of ordinary truth or falsehood: what action or the like will be best in terms of effectiveness and costliness in serving the principle's own end, getting or keeping people out of bad lives? That is not at all the question of whether or not an action maximizes the total of satisfaction or happiness. You could sometimes do that maximizing by making good lives still better, perhaps by accepting a means that actually makes for wretchedness.

Another nearby resistance to consequentialism must call up a very firm reply. It is that *of course* the Principle of Humanity takes more bad lives as worse than fewer bad lives. *Of course* the Principle of Humanity takes an appalling massacre of hundreds to be worse than a single killing. *Of course* the Principle of Humanity takes a stupefying number of deaths by famine to be worse than a few such deaths. *Of course* it takes us to be obliged to choose the least bad upshot.

Is there really anybody, whatever they take to be bad, who doesn't take such a view? Well, some delicate and some tough philosophers have tried to pretend otherwise. They speak in a suspicious way of *any* maximizing principle, as if any such thing had a character repugnant to decent persons. But in fact maximizing, so called, enters into and is the rule in almost all ordinary moral thinking and feeling. It is barely separable from the rationality of taking effective and economical means to an end. If you think abortion is wrong in itself, presumably you want fewer abortions.

Perhaps the real resistance to consequentialism is just a confusion that has to do with that very name given to it, and a description of it that we have gone along with. The name suggests that certain moralities fix their attention on consequences or ends to the exclusion of means, or at least fix their attention more on ends than on means. And if you describe consequentialism as *morality that judges the rightness of things by their anticipated consequences*, you also allow the idea that attention is given to ends rather than means or that too much attention is given to ends.

No doubt there have been some moralities that do this. Mistake and blunder turn up everywhere. But in fact it is absurd to suppose that the Principle of Humanity, for example, does not give full attention to means. On the contrary, full attention to means is explicitly written into it. It specifies from the start what means are all right and what means are not. Means must not be ineffective or self-defeating. In fact the principle is as much concerned with means as ends – both are considered in terms of getting or keeping people out of bad lives.

What the principle does is indeed to take the end and the means to justify the means. It requires that the end and the means together do that.

Could it be that if a philosopher had not attached a name to some moralities, various objections and confusions would have been left behind sooner?

Defining Terrorism

Politicians and spokesmen for the state of Israel were the first to be on television regularly telling us that they as a democracy were engaged in a struggle against terrorism – and that therefore they were indubitably in the right. We knew on each occasion what they were to be taken as against. It was the particular event that day or the day before, maybe the suicide bombing in the restaurant in Tel Aviv.

They were succeeded by Americans on television after 9/11, and again we were in no doubt. The terrorism was the flying of the air-liners into the skyscrapers, killing many people. So with the Spanish and their reports of the deaths in Madrid. Now, after 7/7, and the bombs in the Piccadilly Line train and the other trains and the bus, and then the further actions two weeks later, we in England know what is meant when we hear of terrorism on the evening news.

There was no question in our minds of whether any of the men-tioned attacks was other than terrorism. There is no question about including many things under the word. So too with including other things under another word, maybe the word for an airplane, a bomb or a war. In those cases too, we are certain of instances of the kind of thing in question. That leaves room for a general question in all cases, however.

The question, whether or not difficult, is the general definition of the kind of thing. We can be faced with other particular things such that it is unclear whether they count as bombs, airplanes or trains. They raise the question of a general definition of the kind of thing in question. So with terrorism.

The question is one for the makers of dictionaries. But it is also one for anyone trying to think about particular cases or just one case. So it is a question for us. You can come to think or feel differently about a particular thing by seeing that it is like or unlike other things, in the same category or not, maybe in the same category with things you have had certain feelings about. You can judge a particular thing differently, condemn or justify it differently, indeed understand it differently, by seeing it goes with or does not go with other things, by being reminded.

The business of getting a general definition of anything can be carried forward to their satisfaction by people who bring to bear a leaning, impulse, motive, commitment, passion, plan or plot. This situation is pretty ordinary. A corporation aware of regulations, tax law, subsidies, publicity and possible profits in connection with means of transport may try to get the government to take up a general definition of a thing that serves its interest, indeed an airplane or bomb.

A politician or a government spokesman, as all of us know, may implicitly or explicitly assume or define terrorism to be violence against his side, as distinct from the same sort of violence *by* his side. American presidents exclude from the category of terrorism a lot of the violence in South America, including killing and torturing financed, instigated, commissioned or in fact overseen by the CIA. A politician or anybody else can also make terrorism wrong or monstrous and mad by explicit or implicit definition.

This may lead you to suppose that there is a significant problem about a general conception of terrorism in actual thinking about terrorism, in inquiry or serious argument. You may suppose there is a real problem of a philosophical, linguistic, semantic or other intellectual kind. There is no way, you may say, of deciding between what some philosophers used to call persuasive definitions – definitions aimed at persuading us of something. In fact, insofar as actual thinking is concerned, there is *no* significant problem in the existence of different definitions, in the truth that one government's freedom fighter is the next man's terrorist.

Suppose you have sympathy with or are on the side of people you define in a certain way and as a result call freedom-fighters. Suppose I am against people I define in a certain way and as a result call terrorists or worse. The definitions and names may pick out the same people despite our different implications as to what is to be said for or against them. The different implications, whether or not you take them really to be parts of the meanings of the defined terms, make for no significant problem.

You can state your position, to put it at its strongest, by saying there are no persons who fall under my definition of being a terrorist, and that there are persons who fall under your definition of being a freedom-fighter. You can then argue for your position in any way you want. I can state my position by saying there are no persons who fall under your definition of freedom-fighter, only persons who fall under my definition of terrorist, and then support my cause in whatever way. In order to simplify our inquiry, and keep the facts and values separate, we can also come to an agreement to leave out our different attitudes, and then go on to inquire into what can be said for or against these people.

There is no gain for anyone, not even a politician when thinking, in taking up a definition that is one-sided. That there is no way of deciding between definitions, if or to the extent that is true, doesn't matter when we are thinking about things. So there can be no serious reason for dispute here. There can be no irresoluble conflict when there is nothing to gain. There is no gain or conflict in real argument in defining terrorism, in effect, as something such that it is conceptually impossible that American, British or Israeli soldiers should have a part in it, or something that it is impossible that a poor or a victimized country's patriots can be engaged in it. There is no gain for a political philosopher, a philosopher on a side, as most philosophers are, or for an actual partisan, to deftly or undeftly load a definition.

So – we are in no doubt about most instances of terrorism according to an ordinary usage, and general definitions are essential with respect to particular instances, and self-serving general definitions are commonly assumed or advanced, and these do not significantly trouble actual thinking about the subject, and can be replaced by more convenient ones less likely to give rise to confusion. There is one other preliminary.

The fact of alternative definitions and their unimportance in thinking and inquiry, inquiry as pure as it can be, is not to be confused with something else. It is not the proposition that what is meant and implied in talk of terrorism is unimportant elsewhere. Exactly the opposite is true. The world isn't a university or a book or a half-decent discussion. If it could be, there are people who make sure it isn't.

We live in a world where the very strongest resource in public opposition to the Palestinians, say, is a kind of talk of terrorism. If there is no possibility of defining your way into a moral conclusion worth consideration, there is every possibility of implicitly defining your way into one not worth consideration but of the greatest effect. Say the greatest effect in getting people to take a side, suppose that there is no question at all to be asked about it, go along with policies and actions of the greatest consequence.

That a use or uses of the word *terrorism* became common and entrenched was as much owed to partisan and political intent as anything else – as much owed to politicians keen to have a tool to add to their propaganda as anything else. Before the recent beginning of Islamic and some other violence, incidentally, and as you will remember, the word *terrorism* turned up only in history books, mainly on the French Revolution. Violence of the kind we are considering was known as *political violence*, and conferences on that subject were indeed called conferences on political violence.

The word *terrorism* has been as effective a means as any other, as effective as all but a couple of others, in getting two countries into a war. The Iraq war has killed, according to an arguable estimate, about 60,000 civilians – 60,000. They were individuals with names and girlfriends and husbands, once with as much hope about their lives as Blair, say, or the Brazilian electrician Jean Charles de Menezes known to us all in England after he was mistakenly shot by anti-terrorist police in a London subway station.

But the larger proposition about the effect of a word is not our concern now. To see something more of the nature and size of the problems concerning general definition that do arise in actual thought and inquiry, let us proceed by settling on such a definition for our own inquiry.

Terrorism is first of all violence, a destructive use of force. It includes killing, maiming and destroying, and, as you can reasonably add, the aftermaths of those things. There was once an inclination on the part of progressive and usually Marxist thinkers to widen the understanding of violence further so as to cover what does not itself include physical force. This was exploitation and so on, maybe capitalism. It was given the special name of being structural or institutional violence. We need not join these thinkers. One reason for not doing so is that we would be led away from our chosen subject matter, at any rate led away before time.

Terrorism, secondly, is violence that is smaller in scale than war. We can leave it to others to say how much smaller, draw the line. Whatever else is to be said of the two things, we do want a distinction between 9/11 and war. It may serve us not only in making other differences between the two things but in seeing some sameness. You cannot usefully condemn or defend in a common way what you begin by confusing.

Thirdly, terrorism has a political aim and hence also another aim of a people, what is underdescribed as a social aim. This aim will have to do, certainly, with a people or a country and the great human goods, the fundamental desires shared by all of us. Terrorism is not criminality engaged in for personal gain or indulgence. If it may also be motivated by other things, that is a fact about it shared with virtually all human endeavours. Mixed motivation is consistent with a main motivation, the main motivation of a shared movement.

Fourthly, terrorism is violence that is not according to national or international law. It does not include the lawful violence of police and soldiers. It does not include some national acts, maybe on the way to being just wars. Whatever follows or fails to follow from making terrorism illegal by definition, and whatever difficulties this raises, it is pretty essential to the useful fixing of a subject matter.

Certainly there has to be a difference made for purposes of inquiry between young Muslim men putting bombs on London subway trains and our security forces shooting them. The difference cannot be made in terms of wrong and right, which would beg the question we are considering in these and other cases, maybe harder cases. Also it would make a definition of terrorism into a source of confusion, since there is disagreement as to whether some actions and campaigns were or are wrong, starting with those that resulted in nations coming into being and are now dignified or celebrated.

A decent definition must then make a difference between things in terms of illegality and legality. The policy is followed by definers as different as Chomsky, the US Army, the British government in its Terrorism Act 2000, and presumably the makers of all other effective legal definitions. The policy is not made mistaken by the uncomfortable fact that it follows that terrorism is on the way to being what national states decide it to be – by making national or international law.

Fifthly and finally, however, we can usefully make explicit that terrorism does raise a question of its being wrong, of its being unjustified. Indeed, it is better to go further, and specify that it is *prima facie* wrong, which is implicit in its being killing, maiming, and the ruining of other lives. There is an immediate case against it to be answered. This is to say, no more and as much as would usefully be said in a definition of war.

This definition of terrorism as violence, short of war, political, illegal and *prima facie* wrong, does of course result in questions. The largest does indeed have to do with the requirement that terrorism is not in accordance with national or international law. As we noticed earlier, international law is not a clear and settled thing. Far from it. It quickly drifts off into what can be called norms and conventions, neither of them clearly specifiable. In which case, the given definition of terrorism is vague.

That may strike you as unimportant, since in fact international law is not so unclear and unsettled as to leave a doubt as to whether at least 9/11 or 7/7 consisted in terrorism. And, for purposes of inquiry, we may rule that the Palestinian *intifadas* or uprisings are also to count as terrorism. Indeed I do so. This will surprise no one aware of the fact of decision as against discovery in the process of making definitions. In fact vagueness remains a problem with the definition, but a manageable one. There are worse things about definitions.

It will be clear, with hardly a moment's reflection, that the definition we have does not exclude the possibility of there being terrorism by a national state. It does not exclude the possibility of *state terrorism*, as well called *official terrorism*. Violence by a state can obviously satisfy all the requirements in the definition, most relevantly the one about international law. And there can unquestionably be terrorism by a democratic state.

As, plainly, the definition is not to be understood as carrying any significant implication about war, anything other than that war is larger. It leaves open the possibility that war may be wrong, and that a war against terrorism may be wrong. The definition also leaves open the possibility that war as distinct from terrorism may be against international law or resolutions, or not permitted by them. This war, of course, will also be violence, with a political or social aim, and *prima facie* wrong. It will be useful if we have a name for this kind of war.

It can be *terrorist war*, which is not to imply that it is actually a kind of terrorism as defined, but that it shares the properties of that terrorism other than being relatively small scale. Or it can be *criminal war*, which reminds us that it has a principal property of terrorism, being against law, as well as all the others save for being small scale. Either name is at least as apposite for what it names as *terrorism* is for what it names. Whatever recommendation is had by the use of the term *terrorism* as defined, there presumably is the same recommendation for the use of the term *terrorist war*. So with *criminal war*.

To return to our definition of terrorism, it leaves open more than the possibility of state or official terrorism. As you have heard, despite its attention to the *prima facie* wrongfulness of terrorism, the definition leaves open the possibility of rightful terrorism. Some of it may be democratic terrorism – aimed at the achievement of democracy. This may reassure admirers of Nelson Mandela of the African National Congress, Americans and others who have financed freedom-fighters, and clear-headed patriots of an historical turn of mind of very many nations, including Israel. But the fact is of greater importance than this. The definition in this and its other parts, if it is no more essential to inquiry than any other definition, does serve inquiry. It helps a little to avoid confusion, manipulation, forgetfulness, being led astray by oneself, and so on.

That the definition leaves open the possibility of rightful terrorism goes with something else. The definition also leaves it open, as it must, that an act or campaign of terrorism is also other things. It may be self-defence, resistance, resistance to ethnic cleansing in particular. It may be resistance to genocide, a liberation struggle, a humanly necessary opposition to the vile self-interest of others or another people or their leaders, and more than that.

It is worth noticing, to revert to terrorist war for a minute or two, that this kind of war is like terrorism itself in that it may be right – despite being *prima facie* wrong – and it may be wrong. We are not begging this or any other question in advance. To see or judge that a war is terrorist is not in itself to see or judge that it is wrong. It is not in itself to condemn it. It *is* to do something else important. It is to remove what others may take to be a distinction of this war, a reason or justification for it – the supposed good reason that it is according to law. It is not according to law, whatever justification that would be. This legalism is hopeless.

If this is not familiar thinking or talking about terrorism and war, certainly not the thinking of most of our politicians, it is plainly needed. What it amounts to at bottom is that some war can have all the properties of terrorism except that it is larger in scale, including the property of illegality. That there is not much distinction between them, indeed so little distinction, is an excellent reason for marking their sameness by a name. We need that reminder. And there is the more particular reason that we make it less likely that anyone will fall into the confusion of supposing that since there is always a special kind of defence for war, legality, there is always a special or unique objection to terrorism. There is not.

To harp on a bit, the main fact about each of terrorism and terrorist war and other war as we are understanding them is that each may be wrong and each may possibly be right. So far as our definitions go, then, there can be right terrorism against wrong terrorist war or wrong other war. So far as our definitions go, the terrorism can instead be wrong and the terrorist war or other war right. Our definitions are therefore as they should be for the purposes of thinking and indeed feeling. We are not prejudging, not begging questions. We are avoiding what can be regarded as the intellectual absurdity of these years, maybe of this age, in our part of the world. It is also avoided, incidentally, in good thinking not in terms of the Principle of Humanity but in terms of the just war theory and indeed human rights. In reflective company our way of proceeding is far from unique.

There are indeed other general definitions of terrorism than the one we have. The one that is most in use by our leaders, as you have heard, makes terrorism at least wrong or unjustified, usually evil or monstrous. Terrorism as we have defined it may be all of those things. In the matter of definition, we need have no objection to the judgements and feelings, or indeed engage in a determined opposition to our leaders' definition. We could take up a definition that begins with the one we have and adds to it a final clause to specify that terrorism is wrong or purely evil. This would impede our inquiry somewhat and make it necessary to define another term or two, say one for activity that would be terrorism except that it is not purely evil, and perhaps lead to mistakes by the simple or the merely emotional. But, as you have heard, it would not do more than that.

In part we are in fact inquiring into the right or wrong, the morality or immorality, the humanity or inhumanity, of what is done in Palestine by Palestinians, and by Zionists and neo-Zionists, and what was done on 9/11 and 7/7 and what has been done in Iraq. If we were to take up our leaders' definition of terrorism we would have before us the questions, among others, as they would now be expressed, of whether 9/11 and 7/7 *were* terrorism, and if so, why. They could turn out not to be despite the definition, as noted earlier. The definition itself would complicate but not really affect our inquiry.

The same remark is to be made about another common definition of terrorism. It requires that terrorism is directed against innocents, non-combatants or the like randomly chosen. That verb 'directed' will need real clarification, of course, which will raise problems, but leave that for a while. Suppose the definition under consideration, more exactly, is the one we have settled on ourselves but with that additional clause about innocents or non-combatants.

It goes some way in implying that terrorism is wrong, certainly, since there must be a presumption that killing innocents is wrong – a presumption of the Principle of Humanity in particular. The definition will have inconveniences, presumably. The killing of the commander in chief, the president of the United States, who can hardly be regarded as a non-combatant – the killing of him by a suicide bomber of what is called al-Qaeda – will not be terrorism. But that is of no great importance, partly because all definitions are likely to have inconveniences. It will take a little care, but we could about as well carry forward our inquiry in terms of the definition mentioning innocents or non-combatants, and, of course, also in terms of what we will also need, conceptions of related killings and the like where the victims are not innocents or non-combatants.

Shall we add that terrorism terrifies or causes fear? Well, *war* terrifies, more than any other human activity, more than terrorism.

The effect of defining terrorism as terrifying is to imply mistakenly that it has a character that individuates it, and a character that invites a special abhorrence. It is in effect to invite a kind of *prima facie* approval or tolerance of war, including terrorist war, by means of overlooking *its* nature. If you want to add that terrorism depends more on terror than war depends on terror, I might be content to stick that in along with something else – that terrorism depends greatly less on actual amounts of killing than war does, and maybe that unofficial terrorism kills nothing like as many as state terrorism.

Given all this, how is a definition to be chosen? It is clear how the noticed alternatives to our definition *are* chosen. They are chosen in order to try to beg a question, or predispose us to an answer to the main question. At least they are chosen in order to keep our minds fixed on some considerations rather than others. But is that sort of thing always wrong? In general wrong?

Our own definition of terrorism as violence, smaller-scale than war, political and social, illegal, and *prima facie* wrong has the recommendation of being ordinary, or ordinary when we are *thinking* about our subjects, asking certain questions with minds as open as they can be. It is not a definition that can recommend itself in some places at some times. It did not recommend itself on days of horror, 9/11 or 7/7, or the days just afterwards. It can recommend itself now. It has the recommendation of fixing a subject matter unconfusingly, distinguishing it from nearby ones, and not excluding those other subject matters.

That is not all that can be thought about, however. You may think, not absurdly, to go back to the question of a moment ago, that getting the right and the human answer to questions of terrorism is of such importance that you must insist on a definition that helps us all on the way. You must insist, you say, on a definition that includes the random killing of innocents.

You know it will not help much and it will not help at all with someone who is clear-headed and resolute about coming to the right answer himself. He can easily conclude, no matter the definition, that some terrorism as defined by you is, say, on a level with killing non-innocents, maybe that some of the killing of non-innocents is worse. You cannot prevent conclusions by definitions. Still, you say, the right definition may do some good.

I do not much mind admitting that my definition of terrorism may owe something to my commitment to the Principle of Humanity, as you have heard. It does not allow us to suppose or to drift towards supposing that it is only terrorism that kills innocent people. It does not distract us from the fact that war does. It does not make a difference between terrorism and war that does not exist. To define terrorism in a way that does not contribute to toleration of killing innocents in war is to be more effectively against killing innocents than somebody who defines terrorism as against innocents and thus *does* contribute to toleration of the killing of *more* innocents.

So my definition may do some good. It may also do some good in other respects, say in making automatism about terrorism and democracy less likely. To what is your definition owed, by the way? Where does it come from? You can think more about that when we come back to the subject, which we will.

Palestine

Various ways of coming to judgements of right and wrong about Palestine, 9/11, Iraq and 7/7 have been contemplated. We have looked at negotiation to the exclusion of all else, international law, United Nations resolutions, human rights, just war theory, the politics of reality, conservatism, liberalism, and our democracy as it is.

Despite the use in reflection and judgement of the UN resolutions, human rights, and just war theory, these alternatives to the Principle of Humanity have been a large side of the argument for the principle, an argument from comparison. The relative uncertainty or the failure of these alternatives is not less important than what else has been said on behalf of the morality of humanity. In that morality, summed up by its principle, we do have a foundation for judgements, and indeed more than that.

We have a general line of argument towards answers to all the questions of right and wrong that are our subject. It is reassuring that there is a human convergence on roughly this morality. It is not the idea of a philosopher. What a philosopher brings to it is organization and defence – the aspiration to logic of which you heard in the beginning. Also some empathy and some resolution that can grow out of that logic, along with a scepticism.

I myself am tempted to go further – despite needing to keep in mind that you may value one of those alternative ways of coming to judgements more than me, and that a full account and defence of the morality of humanity has not been completed. I am tempted to suppose that what has been completed and could be enlarged is not the harder part of our inquiry, but the the easier. The temptation is to think that what is hardest about morality, so to speak, is not morality. What is hardest are questions of fact, questions of ordinary truth rather than moral truth.

Any line of argument, any attempt at logic with respect to a question, say the question of Palestine, necessarily depends on and is informed by a general moral view. But the line of argument also depends on beliefs as to fact or more likely something less certain than judgements of fact. These, it can seem, are harder to arrive at than the moral view. A prime example of this difficulty is the question of whether an alternative to some particular past campaign of terrorism, say negotiation, would have worked out better. Another prime example, more pressing, is whether terrorism now will secure a certain end or one of a range of ends, or will instead be the worst of things – useless killing, useless suffering, useless wrecking of lives.

There is also a different kind of difficulty, also familiar. This is not in general about probability. It is about the selection of facts, a selection from history or from the contemporary scene. We can have the aim of making a balanced selection that gives attention to the claims as to relevance of Palestinians on the one hand and Zionists and neo-Zionists on the other. We can also have the aim, see the necessity, of judging for ourselves, if uncertainly. It needs remembering that there aren't two sides to be considered with a real rape. There aren't two sides to that story.

These factual difficulties make the connection between the basic moral view and particular conclusions of right and wrong, say about Palestine, less than tight. Certainly there is no simple deduction between the Principle of Humanity and the particular conclusions. This is of course the circumstance of all of us, of whatever morality. We can be reassured by the fact, however, that there *is* the possibility of well-argued connection, and that all of us must depend on it in dealing with our existence. You cannot give up on trying to answer inescapable questions because they are not geometry.

Factual judgements with respect to Palestine must begin with the past. Not for the past itself, but because the past does or does not result in or make for desires in the present, desires rightly said to be needs. The past validates or does not validate claims about the existence of desires or needs. For a group of persons each with such desires and specially related by them – a people – to claim a land as a means to their having certain of the great goods is for them to have to show, so to speak, the size of the harm of the denial of these goods to them, which harm depends in large or considerable part on their past.

Palestine as an historic territory had an ancient and later history that was more a matter of empires such as the Persian and the Roman than local or indigenous peoples and kingdoms. With respect to the local peoples and kingdoms, necessarily our concern, the run of history over centuries, despite the episodes in the Bible, has had more ascendancy by Arab and mainly Muslim peoples. The centuries have been greatly more Arab than Jewish. The Arabs, partly on account of having remained in Palestine, can with reason be said to be the indigenous people.

To those propositions of fact, another needs to be added. It is that ancient history is indeed just ancient history. It is what doesn't really matter any more. Also, all history before the time of the grand-parents of those alive is not greatly more real than ancient history in the lives of a people. Claims to the contrary about the ancient past or the other less real past, although feelingful, can reasonably be taken as mainly pretences. Who for a moment, when not out for gain by any means in argument, puts feelingful thoughts about the ancient and the other unreal past in the same scale with separate thoughts about the great human goods and being denied them now?

So take instead the last quarter of the century before the one with 1948 in it, a quarter of a century with some grandparents in it. Around 1875, there were in Palestine more or greatly more than 25 Palestinians, the very great majority of them Muslims, for every one Jewish person. Palestine was Palestinian.

Anti-semitism elsewhere, mainly in Eastern Europe, then resulted in Jewish immigration. After the end of World War 1 and the collapse of the Ottoman Empire, the territory became a British pro-tectorate under a mandate of the League of Nations. There were still more than thirteen Palestinians for every Jewish person.

The anti-semitism elsewhere also resulted in the rise of Zionism understood as an historical movement towards the establishing of some or other Jewish homeland, a Jewish homeland of some or other extent, in Palestine. This historical Zionism is distinct from something else you have been hearing of from me, Zionism defined as the defence and justification of the existence of Israel within its original 1948 borders.

Zionism of that latter kind is evidently a clear subject matter, and excludes no other subject matter from consideration. Also, it carries no implication whatever as to the plans, intentions, hopes and no doubt plots of Zionism in the other and more historical sense. It is in fact impossible to believe that anything like all of historical Zionism had small ambitions with respect to Palestine, indeed any commitment to sharing that land. Those who condemn it, notably Jews, have reason to speak of ethnic nationalism, a movement of racial supremacy, that was by no means moderate in its ambitions. But the matter does not affect the clear use of the term in our sense.

It is important, to continue the story, that there was considerable opposition to the Jewish immigration and to historical Zionism by Palestinian nationalists. They existed and they were fearful for the future. This organized opposition included attempts at international persuasion as well as demonstrations, strikes, riots and what were called pogroms.The Balfour Declaration in 1917, by the British Foreign Minister of that name, supported the idea of a national homeland for the Jews in Palestine but also stated that 'nothing shall be done which may prejudice the civil and religious rights of existing non-Jewish communities in Palestine'.

The greatest suffering of a single people in the twentieth century was the killing of something like six million Jews by the German state during World War 2. There was some knowledge of this on the part of the German people, and no significant resistance. The Holocaust also carried with it humiliation and fear, indeed a denial of all that gives value to human life. It was a manufacturing of what it is insufficient to call bad lives.

No explanation of the Holocaust, in terms of the natures and activities of both non-Jews and Jews, no reasonable idea about exaggeration in connection with the Holocaust, no carelessness about who else died in it, no anti-semitism or Jewish self-criticism, can reduce the overwhelming force of this fact. Nothing makes it less than monstrous.

There is something smaller, if significant, that is now about as clear. It is that at the end of the war, a homeland for the Jewish people ought to have been created out of Germany. It was not the Palestinians who voted for Hitler in a German democracy and then ran the death camps. It was not the Palestinians who for conclusive reasons, quite separate from retribution, should have given more than help to the Jews, more than compensation. It is Germany, beyond question of doubt, out of which a homeland for the Jews ought to have been carved.

A further thing is now as significant and as clear. It is that such a thing was not at the end of the war conceived as a possibility. The right place for a Jewish homeland and sanctuary could not be thought. It was not only not within any range of options in fact considered, but, so to speak, was not a conceivable option. I leave it to others to reflect on the explanation of this fact. That it was a fact, that something did not exist in thinking and feeling, and hence that a possibility did not exist in the world, seems beyond question.

To this absence in thought and hence in reality of a possibility has to be added something that *was* present in both thought and reality, a kind of necessity. After Belsen and Buchenwald, it was a human necessity that *some* homeland for the Jews come into being. What I have in mind, as you may guess, is a kind of fact of somehow human and factual necessity as distinct from what there also was, a moral necessity. That the fact is not clear does not make it less than a fact.

To return to Palestine, there was very large Jewish immigration into it just before, during and of course after World War 2. This resulted in there being not about 25 or 13 Arabs for each Jewish person in Palestine but about 2.3.

The state of Israel was brought into being in the land of Palestine in 1948, partly by means of Jewish terrorism, some of it led by a subsequent prime minister of the state. In the Israeli share of Palestine, there were about as many Arabs as Jews. In the Palestinian share of Palestine, where no state was formed, there were about 80 times as many Palestinians as Jews.

Palestinians of course fought against those who were dispossessing them. What happened, nonetheless, as we have all been led into the habit of saying, was that there was *partition* of the land. Many of us have supposed, and some still do, that a part or maybe something like a half of the land went to each people. In fact at the end of a struggle the Jewish people had acquired from the Palestinians about 80 per cent of Palestine. They took much more than was laid down by a UN resolution. That figure of about 80 per cent of the land needs keeping in mind. As you have heard, there were still more than twice as many Palestinians.

This was for the Palestinians the Nakbah, the catastrophe. In a large way, it denied most of them most of the great human goods and to all of them several. Many hundreds of thousands of Palestinians were expelled or fled from their towns, villages, houses, olive groves and pasts in what was now Israel. They became refugees in grim or appalling camps.

This, called *transfer*, was indubitably what became known later in the twentieth century as ethnic cleansing. What was lacking was television or maybe, after the war, the strength to attend to a thing. It is as correct to speak of ethnic cleansing as it was to speak of olive groves. Israel leaders spoke of the need to 'clean' the country.

But the founding of the state of Israel was not owed only to immigration, the Holocaust, the non-existence of a possibility as to a homeland in Germany, the human necessity of a Jewish homeland – and also the international campaign of historical Zionism, probably some English anti-semitism, and certainly Jewish terrorism. It was also owed to another fact about as large as the non-possibility and the necessity.

The Palestinians, although they had fought against the occupation of their land, had not formed themselves into a state. They had not separated themselves from other Arabs. They were those who lived in a place, the place with their name, the place most recently defined by way of the British protectorate. But they did not have *their* borders. They did not have the means of affirming a freedom, a unity in relationship, a culture and a past that is exactly a national state.

Those truths come together into one proposition. The Palestinians were *not fully a people*. What I mean is that it was not ignorant and it was within reason to judge in 1948 and before that the Palestinians were not fully a people. No doubt the judgement can still be taken as condescending and offensive. It could be judged, nonetheless, on the basis of respectable belief and reasonable thinking, that the Palestinians for clear reasons lacked the self-consciousness of a people. It was possible to believe as fairly, too, that they did not have a general will as a people.

It followed, as the most important thing, whatever needed to be admitted in qualification of it, that the Palestinians could not suffer an overwhelming kind of catastrophe. They could not have the pain and suffering of being deprived of a certain kind of the great goods of freedom and power, relationship, respect and self-respect, and culture – that kind that depends exactly on a realized fact of relationship, being fully a people in their own land. There was a way in which they did not have great goods taken from them.

It is a good idea to hurry to say that none of this had to be confused in 1948 or was confused with a vicious piece of rhetorical nonsense, never believed by the historical Zionists who used it. This was that there was a land without people waiting there, into which there could come a people without a land, the Jews. There were people there, all right, and they knew who they were, and everybody else knew who they were, even if they had not become a further thing.

There is more to be said of this Palestinian condition of the founding of Israel, this judgement about the Palestinians not being fully a people. We will be coming back to it. Now, let us complete a history, or rather bring it up to date. This has to do with the 1967 war, and the subsequent control of and expansion of Israel into more of Palestine, and the further resistance of the Palestinians, and the lives of the Jewish people in Israel.

The explanation of the starting of the brief war in 1967 cannot be much disputed by non-partisans. It was less a pre-emptive attack by the Israelis, a response to true and immediate danger, than aggression by way of a pretence of believing something about an imminent attack. Was it a terrorist war? I suppose so, but there is a little room for dispute, and I do not press my answer on you.

Israel was well prepared for the war and won it easily in six days. This had very much to do with what would become a whole history of financial and other support by Jews in America and the American government. This support, not only owed to Jewish influence and power in America, but also American self-interest with respect to the Middle East and oil, was to be an essential part in what followed. The history of Palestine is partly in America, partly in New York, Los Angeles and Washington. Right or wrong in Palestine is importantly American right or wrong, almost as much by commission as by omission.

That is to say, more particularly, that the United States has had a large part in neo-Zionism. It has had a large part, that is, in the fact and the supposed justification of the expansion of Israel after 1967 beyond its original borders, or more or less its original borders, with what this has involved and continues to involve for the Palestinians. There are now several million Palestinian refugees. Hundreds of thousands of Jews have come to Israel from Russia and elsewhere.

What neo-Zionism has come to, whether pursued by hawks or doves in Israeli politics, to speak differently, is a determination by way of a kind of democratic government to take possession in perpetuity of more of the remaining 20 per cent of the land of the Palestinians, and control of all of it. This needs to be kept in view. Neo-Zionism is the determination, after 80 per cent of what is properly described as the land of another people has already been taken, to take at least some of the rest.

To this can be added what is less important, which is that neo-Zionism has been and is terrorism. Putting aside the somewhat disputed 1967 war itself, neo-Zionism has been and is terrorism by a national state. Its attacks, killings, maimings, destructions and depradations of every kind could be nothing else. Look back to the definition of terrorism. With respect to the clause about international law, look back to the earlier account of the UN resolutions and the Declaration of Human Rights, and even to the preceding account of international law in general. Neo-Zionism is violence, somewhat smaller scale than war, with a political aim, not according to international law, and *prima facie* wrong. There is no possibility of questioning this conclusion.

As for the Palestinians, given the aggression against them and the further occupation of their homeland since 1967, their defence of themselves is unquestionably far *less* open to the judgement that it is terrorism. It is not the *intifadas* or uprisings that more certainly are terrorism. This turns again on the requirement for terrorism that it be against international law.

Are you a reader who is surprised, taken aback, suspicious, superior, disbelieving, dismissive or outraged with respect to the judgement that a sovereign state, a member of the United Nations, a government with a place among governments and with the special support of the United States of America, a country, an elected leadership of a people of distinction over centuries – is definitely terrorist? And as surprised or whatever by the idea that HAMAS and the suicide-bombers are less terrorist?

If so, I again say consider what you very likely took to be at the very least a useful description of terrorism, and consider again those other things just mentioned, above all the UN resolutions. There is nothing contentious or merely arguable or unrealistic about taking neo-Zionist Israel to be terrorist. Consider too the matter of your being subject to a convention of thought and attitude in a society. Consider whether you are to think and feel as Blair or Bush seek to have you think and feel. Or Murdoch or Fox TV or Sharon. You have followed a line of inquiry or argument, good or bad. I guess you thought about it and that you can still think about it without them.

But if not, that is no matter. Start again with their definition or your own. It will change no facts, improve no argument. We are trying to reason here, not condemning by defining, not ranting, wailing, speechifying, or winning approval by means of mildness or decorum.

Two other things are in need of consideration. One is the resistance of the Palestinians to neo-Zionism and to the power that is the United States. This liberation struggle, this struggle for independence, has been a thing that gives as much cause for reflection as the founding of Israel. Are there precedents of this resistance elsewhere in history? It must be reasonable to describe the *intifadas* as unprecedented. Against overwhelming power, against money, missiles and the propaganda of denigration, against decades of humiliation and degradation, the Palestinians have endured, continued to claim what their humanity entitles them to, suffered, and died. They have not given up.

About 3,300 of them have been killed, including a significant number of children, as against about 975 Israelis.

Against tanks they have fought first with slings and stones. Against everything, they have then fought with the sacrifice of their lives. Young men and women have died and killed for their people, because of their people. They have certainly not died and killed *because* of a real or contemplated belief in immortality. Certainly they have been martyrs for their people. No talk about democracy and terrorism, no contumely, no racism, can touch this human reality. Their struggle against a denial of human goods, a kind of struggle sacred in a sense that does not have to do with religion but rather sacred in being rightly reverenced, is one such fact that will be of importance to our conclusions about Palestine.

The other thing for you to consider is the people of the state of Israel. That state, as you may anticipate I believe, has become vicious. It is a violator of another people, a nuclear power and the fourth greatest military power in the world pretending to be a victim. It has clearly had the policy of avoiding a negotiated peace settlement with the Palestinians, which settlement would be subject to a little international influence, in order to gain more land for itself. It is a kind of ethnic democracy, arguably racist, perhaps better called a near-democracy, one that discriminates legally against the Palestinians still in Israel.

But that is perfectly consistent with something else, quite as large a fact.

It is that Israel is now also the homeland of the Jews. A half-century has passed since 1948. A homeland has come into being. Its human existence is a reality entirely independent of whatever can be said of an ancient past. It has come into being and lives of Jewish people are in it, including the lives of many so honourably and courageously opposed to the neo-Zionism of their state. They have human rights there. They can weep too. Something of the lives of many Jews who are not there is also there.

Whatever was true and right in 1948, a matter of judgement to which we are coming, the lives of the Jews in Israel are now deep in a land. Their identity is there, their desires, their hopes. So is the past that was the Holocaust. They have now endured where they are. Their great goods as a people are there. They have escaped discrimination there. Their self-respect, their relationships and their culture are bound up in or with the place. There is sacredness in this fact too.

Further, if there is no argument of weight that Zionism could depend on in connection with an ancient past, no argument of the weight of one that has to do with the great human goods in their fullness, and no such argument at all for neo-Zionism, and if there has been pretence about the ancient past, there is something else that is consistent with all of this. It is at least the relevance of a kind of attachment to the place owed to the content of Jewish religion and culture that has to do with the ancient past. Myth itself is not irrelevant to the matter.

That is not all. It would be invidious to deny to the Jews the pride of being a singular people, the pride of being singular contributors to the culture of us all, a pride that calls for a place. At the head of their ranks of contributors, you can say, if you are of my mind, are Maimonides, Spinoza, Marx, Mendelssohn, Proust, Frankfurter, Schoenberg, Miller, Salk and Chomsky.

Time changes things. It has. Time since 1948 has changed things. This too will be of importance to our conclusions.

Some Conclusions about Palestine

We have the stuff of a line of argument, at bottom a moral principle and a morality, and we also have an account of relevant facts. I myself have some but not a lot of doubt of either. A number of conclusions of the line of argument can be stated quickly.

The founding of the state of Israel in 1948 was right. It then had the only justification that matters, a moral justification. It has to be allowed, against this, that what was done, despite a concord of nations, was more against than in accord with international law, unquestionably international law in the making.

The founding of the state also included terrorism, *prima facie* wrong. It was, greatly more importantly, a violation of the Palestinians. Therefore there was, from the point of view of the Principle of Humanity, a great argument against it. But there also was, from the Principle of Humanity, a yet greater argument for this means to a Jewish state within the original borders. In my view, arguably, the terrorism of Zionism was justified, right.

The argument for the state of Israel and the terrorism has in it, as you know, the Holocaust, the inconceivability of a homeland for the Jews in Germany, the necessity of a homeland for them somewhere, and the proposition in 1948, a matter of the available knowledge and judgement, that the Palestinians were not fully a people and so could not have the suffering of being denied a singular kind of great goods.

A second conclusion is also a conclusion for Zionism. It has to do, however, not with what was the case in 1948. It has to do, rather, with the lives of the Jewish people within the original Israel over half a century since 1948. Those lives have grown and are rooted there, I say again, and have a dependence on that land. This is a human fact that has a kind of sacredness that is not a fact of religion.

It issues in the judgement that the security and perpetuity of Israel within its original borders has a justification, on grounds of what has happened since 1948, as definite as the justification of the founding of Israel in 1948. If it were possible to contemplate bringing the state of Israel to an end, to manufacture more bad lives, it would be morally absurd to do so. You will gather that this can be taken as a proposition independent of the Holocaust and of what else was true or taken as true in 1948. It is a proposition qualified only by the truth that many hundreds of thousands of Palestinians made into refugees must have at least the fullest compensation for having their places of living taken from them. They have a claim comparable to the claim of the Jews against the Germans, whatever other comparisons do or do not hold.

To these judgements for Zionism is to be added as confident a judgement against neo-Zionism. This follows, as you will know I believe, from the morality we have taken up, and from the history of Palestine. Neo-Zionism has been wrong. It has been viciously wrong. It has been a rapacious violation of a people. It is correct that it should have been led by a war criminal, Sharon, the effective murderer of the refugees in the refugee camps of Sabra and Shatila, as good as judged so by his own people. Neo-Zionism, further, has been a thing that could and now has contributed to a more terrible war, one in Iraq.

You will have taken in before now that neither morality nor thinking about it are simple. They are not simple despite the existence of moral truth. Here is a further complexity for you. It is persuasive to say that the wrong of neo-Zionism follows as a conclusion from the morality we have taken up and the history of Palestine. It is as persuasive to say, it seems, that the wrong of neo-Zionism stands as a given, something that can as much begin a work of inquiry as be confirmed in the course of it, confirmed by a principle. Mutual support is somehow the story.

About Zionism and neo-Zionism, incidentally, you now have my main reasons for having distinguished between them from the beginning, taken care about two definitions, departed from a commoner usage. It is possible to speculate that partisans on both sides of the Palestinian conflict see something to gain from talking only of Zionism, and allowing the term to cover both of the things we have distinguished. That is, they use the term vaguely for more or less what we have put aside as historical Zionism – a movement towards the establishing of some or other Jewish state, of some size or other, in Palestine.

Palestinian partisans, knowing most of the world's view of neo-Zionism, give it a name that also covers our defined Zionism, thereby extending the feeling against the former to the latter. Sabra and Shatila come together with and condemn the founding of Israel. Jewish partisans, knowing of the same feeling against neo-Zionism, give it a name that associates it with something different, our Zionism. The decency of the founding of Israel comes to the aid of the barbarism of Sabra and Shatila. We need our distinction. There is a difference that needs marking.

I come now not yet to the further conclusions of right or wrong about Palestine, but rather to another matter of fact. It has to do first with a proposition of which you know, that the Palestinians were not fully a people in 1948. There is use for some moral philosophy in considering this matter and what follows from it.

A question of right or wrong at a time, as has been at least implicit in all you have heard, is always relative to the best information and judgement then available. As remarked earlier, what is right according to the Principle of Humanity has to do with the course of action that can be taken as rational in the sense of being an effective and economical means to an end. What is right, more particularly, is the course of action that is the rational one according to the best knowledge and judgement available.

So what is right at any time depends on what can then be found out and best weighed. Do you doubt this? Do you think rightness is somehow independent of these things? Consider an example.

Suppose the best knowledge and experience is utilized in a woman's decision to leave her money in her will to a particular institute of cancer research. This is the place that on all the evidence must be taken as the most promising. It happens, however, in the course of time, because of the money, that the institute's research throws up some mutation or plague that takes a multitude of lives horribly. Was the wrong thing done back then when the money was given to the institute? Surely not. The right thing was done then, and it happened that the right decision turned out badly, catastrophically.

Of course something else can be said at the later time. You can say that from the later perspective, when things had turned out badly, the act of philanthropy has to be seen as not right but wrong. But it remains the case that the philanthropy was right in what may be the fundamental sense. The act when it was performed was then the best thing that could happen in terms of what was then known and best judged. It is important that the philanthropy was right in the sense that carries the actor's moral credit rather than discredit with it.

Come round now to Palestine. The Holocaust, the unthinkable

about a Jewish homeland in Germany, a human necessity of a homeland, and a reasonable view of the Palestinians – those things made the founding of Israel in Palestine and the terrorism for it right in what is arguably the most fundamental sense. Those who enabled it to happen cannot possibly have our moral disapproval now. They cannot come to have it if it turns out that a mistake was made. They cannot be held responsible, condemned, as a result of something only found out or judged later.

But if something can indeed be right on the basis of what turns out to be a mistake, it is worth adding that rightness on the basis of mistake can be of importance to later judgements. That there was a mistake can be important. Go back for a moment to the woman who made her will, and what followed. Someone else later, knowing the rest of the story, might think differently about a will or something else. They might take a different thing as wise or right than they would have without the earlier case. In a different story but also with a mistake in it, the matter of further and special compensation might come up.

To repeat once more, the founding of Israel in an Arab and mainly Muslim homeland was what ought in 1948 to have happened. There was a moral obligation on the world to forward it, in the state of things then. That is consistent, however, with another judgement to be made today. This, given the best knowledge and judgement now, is that the founding of the state of Israel in Palestine was wrong. That it was wrong has to do with a mistake of fact made in 1948. The Palestinians were *not* as we then thought. They have proved they were otherwise by their subsequent struggle. They have proved this overwhelmingly so by their struggle, since the 1967 war, against the neo-Zionist occupation and control of what remains of their land.

They have proved by their sacrifices that it was *not* the case that in 1948 they were *not fully a people*. It was not the case that they *did not have the self-consciousness of a people*. It was not the case that they *lacked a general will as a people*. Therefore they could and did suffer an overwhelming kind of catastrophe owed to deep relationship, a deprivation of a singular kind of great goods. By their sacrifices, they have proved that they must have been fully a people. They did not come out of a hat later. They were not created as a people by neo-Zionism. A people is not *created*, agreeable as the idea may be to those with a taste for historical drama. That the Palestinians had been and were fully a people was what gave rise to their resistance.

Their struggle has also showed other things of importance to a judgement about it to which we are coming. One is that their struggle proved itself to have been necessary to their having a chance of justice. That it has produced so very little has surely established that anything less would have produced nothing. Their struggle in its resolution, surely, has also established something else. It is that they will succeed in the end. The Palestinians will not give up and they will achieve what they otherwise would not achieve, their country. Not much of a country, but more than has been on offer to them in the false negotiations overseen by America, the offer of a dog's breakfast of bantustans without control of its own borders, not a state at all.

To this certainly can be added something else for those who lack my faith. In World War 2, Jews in the Warsaw ghetto fought to the end. They fought hopelessly, it is still said. They could not hope to live. They bring to mind that there can be a realism in what is hopeless. You can fight, rightly, not for yourself or your time, but for those who come after you. The Jews did so. The Palestinians can do so.

Let us now contemplate the possibility of a certain judgement about the terrorism of the Palestinians as it has been within historic Palestine, including Israel. It would be a judgement owed to all you have heard, including what you have heard of something that was right but owed to a mistake, a mistake seen later. The terrorism of the Palestinians is unquestionably unlike the terrorism of the neo-Zionists.

Are we to judge, to conclude, that it is not to be condemned? That this terrorism of the Palestinians has been right? That this terrorism that has also been self-defence, resistance to ethnic cleansing, self-preservation, the preservation of the existence of a people, a humanly necessary opposition to the excessive self-interest of others, has been justified? That the suicide bombers have been morally permitted if not obliged to do what they have done?

Could it be that the terrorism of the Palestinians, as they have carried it forward until now inside what was Palestine, has been their *moral right*? And that they have this moral right still? To say they have a moral right to their terrorism, as in the case of all claims to moral rights, would be to say that what they have done has been justified or permissible or right, and moreover that this judgement has the support of an entrenched or formidable moral principle. The principle would be that of Humanity.

A Terrible Conclusion about Palestinian Terrorism

Think of the killing of an Israeli child by a Palestinian suicide-bomber. Think too of the shooting to death of a Palestinian child by an Israeli soldier, or the killing of a Palestinian child by an Israeli officer in a helicopter gunship. The soldier has a story, as you will expect. And no doubt the officer in the gunship also says that he would have chosen, if he could, to kill only the HAMAS terrorist in the same street as the child. The Palestinian suicide-bomber, of course, says effectively the same sort of thing, presumably as truly. She would have chosen to have tried as effectively, if she could have, without killing the Israeli child, to save her people.

No such piece of self-justification or justification by others makes the proposition we are contemplating, that the Palestinians have had a moral right to their terrorism, other than terrible. You may say that this very fact of our response to the conclusion cannot be disregarded. You may say this in itself must be a datum or something close to that. Are we wrong then even to reflect on the proposition?

Should we draw that conclusion in advance?

In a way we share a certain reluctance to say any killing is right. In some of us it is stronger – an aversion or recoil with respect to the idea, a determination to deny or condemn it. This human fact is not just the vested interest of politicians in their non-violent line of life. Ordinary attitudes of this kind must have some kind of sympathy from the Principle of Humanity. That is not to say that they can always be supported by it. Maybe they cannot be supported by it with respect to Palestinian self-defence. Does this separate the principle from ordinary morality, divorce it from our lives, make it inhuman?

In fact, whatever the importance of this fact, the proposition that the Palestinians have been right to kill as they have is in a way not extraordinary. Nor would the addition of the claim of a moral right. In a way the terrible answer to the question of right and wrong would not be unusual at all. There is *an* ordinariness about both kinds of claim.

The terrible answer to the question of the right or wrong of neo-Zionist killing is given more or less daily by neo-Zionists, sometimes overtly, more often covertly. They say their killing is right. This is in fact the burden of what is regularly said by neo-Zionist spokesmen and supportive journalists in whatever country. It is given not only when the word 'right' and the like are used, which sometimes they are. It is also given when it is said evasively, to choose one of several examples, that the neo-Zionist killing is somehow *necessary*.

This cannot mean that neo-Zionists literally have no choice. It cannot mean that the age of determinism or Calvinist predestination has arrived in Tel-Aviv, that they have no free will there. It cannot mean that there is somebody or something that really is compelling or constraining Sharon to do things against his will. It is obvious that what must be meant by talk of necessity is that the neo-Zionist killing is along the lines of what you can call a moral necessity, something unavoidable in a right or justified cause. It is certainly not being conceded that the killing is necessary in the course of something wrong or merely selfish, let alone in a crime against humanity.

Neo-Zionist terrorism is often enough defended in terms of Jewish religion. It is sometimes still said, as it was by the German philosophers Hegel and Kant, that Judaism depends on law and revelation, in part religious law. Let us suppose so. Is this sort of law *moral* in character? In that case, it issues in judgements of exactly moral rights and obligations, including judgements about the right-fulness of neo-Zionist terrorism. Is the law somehow other than moral? In that case, exactly like the positive law of a land, it clearly needs the justification of moral principle if it is to be relied on. Then, with that supplement, it again issues in judgements of exactly moral rights and obligations.

There is a simpler thought about the commonness of claims that terrorism is right. It is allowed on all hands that there is a behavioural test of what someone believes and wants. In the long run, the test works better than any other, certainly better than what he or she says she believes and wants. Is there a behavioural test of what someone *believes to be right*? Despite obvious reasons for doubt, I think there is – partly because believing something to be right almost always at least enters into an all-in or inclusive judgement or a final judgement about what is to be done, such a judgement as is indeed revealed best by behaviour.

But there is no need to depend on either the point about law or the point about behaviour. There exists, plainly, the human fact that all of us generally justify what we do. Criminals do so, often by saying we in our societies are all the same, that we are all only out for ourselves, different merely in who gets caught or who makes the rules. The general human fact that we take what we do as right – at least permitted – cannot be missing from Tel-Aviv. We do not need Netanyahu on television to demonstrate the fact.

The terrible proposition of a Palestinian moral right that we are contemplating is not ordinary only when the counterpart claims for neo-Zionist terrorism are considered. If there is a convention of thought and feeling already remarked on, that makes the proposition of a Palestinian moral right seem extraordinary, there is a clear history of such assertions by us all.

We British, not only our propagandists, took it and said that the war against Hitler was right. Many Germans said from their side that the war against us was right. So with the Americans and the war against Japan. It is very relevant that these wars, like more or less all others, had the blessings of the institution of religion. They had the justification by national churches, nothing other than what are often taken as the source of moral decision and instruction.

In World War 2 the terror-bombing of Germany, as indeed it was known, was intended exactly as much to kill civilians as to defeat Hitler. That is what terror-bombing was. This terrorist war-making, this part of World War 2, was justified to us by our leaders. A little later we also took it and said, and have kept on doing so, that the atom bombing of Hiroshima, the killing of very many non-combatants, was justified. So too, to look into the distant past, with the genocide that went with the growth of the United States of America. So too with the murdering of British captives by the terrorists who were serving the justified cause of the founding of the state of Israel after the Holocaust. To this sort of thing other sorts can be added, not irrelevant. There is the fact of the execution of ordinary criminals, the killing of them, not in the past but now, in the United States and elsewhere.

The degree of usualness of the assertion of terrible propositions, including the proposition of neo-Zionists today, is not being remarked on in order to engage in the weakness of *tu quoque* or 'you-too' argument. The usualness does show that asserting the proposition of the moral right of the Palestinians would not divorce the Principle of Humanity from a side of ordinary morality, take it out of sight of life as we live it. The usualness also shows something else.

Moral argument, moral argument in the real world, depends to some extent on what we take other people to think and feel, at least some other people some of the time. We do appeal to their judgements in the way that we have some trust in a sensible jury. A moral claim of a sort never heard of before has less to be said for it. It has its uniqueness to be held against it. A moral claim of a less uncommon sort, in a kind of accord with our human nature, is different. The Palestinians and many who support them morally are not monsters. There are too many people driven to such judgements in the world, far too many, for any to have the rarity of a monster.

The ordinariness of justifications of killing, however, is more important in still another way. It is the fact that it is unquestionable that we regularly go against our aversion or determined resistance to killing. We escape our human reluctance. It is far from being true that we accept a fully general principle against killing. It must then be the case that particular cases and kinds of killing are to be justified or condemned on particular grounds, by way of particular arguments. It must be asked, too, if our resistance to stating moral support for the Palestinian *intifadas* is owed not to reasons, but to something you have heard of before now. That is convention, in particular an unexamined way of thinking and feeling about much terrorism, a way of benefit to some.

There is a need for moral argument in the light of another fact. States and governments, despite the indubitable exceptions that have been noted, often do abide by the practice of avoiding the open or explicit justifying of killing. That is not to say they have nothing to say. What they have to say on many occasions, rather, in one way or another, is in part that some killing has a certain *legitimacy* or *certification*. What this comes to, in full, is that a policy or campaign or war has a legitimacy of which the implication is that the thing is right, very likely obligatory. The legitimacy most commonly claimed in our societies, predictably, is that the policy or whatever is that which has been determined by the leaders of a democracy. Another legitimacy is the supposed thinking and feeling of decent people.

It is part of a decent morality, however, and certainly the obligation of the morality of humanity, to test the implication of states and governments. In effect we did some of that earlier in reflecting on our hierarchic democracies. Another response to the inference from legitimacy to judgements of right and wrong is to ask for explicitness in the support of the judgements. Not allusion to their source and standing but an account of what has convinced the leaders or the decent people. One way of making this demand is to be explicit yourself in saying what you can judge to be right.

I myself am moved by yet another fact of argument that seems as large.

I put aside anyone who takes the view that the Palestinian people do not have a moral right to a *viable national state of their own* – as against, say, the dog's breakfast of a non-state mentioned earlier and supposed to have been on offer to them in the Camp David talks arranged by President Clinton in 2000. It is worth remarking that even the present president of the United States, the younger Bush, a slow learner, has lately come to the view that the Palestinian people do have such a right – thereby vindicating, by the way, the departure of Yasser Arafat from the negotiations at Camp David. Join me, if only for purposes of reflection, in this proposition that the Palestinians do have a moral right to a viable state, whether or not you agree with me that this conclusion is best explained by way of the Principle of Humanity.

In general, can you assert someone's moral right to something and deny that person's moral right to the only possible means to that thing, the necessary means? It is important to have the question clear, and not to engage in loose thinking about moral rights. It is the question of whether you can assert that it is right and justified that someone gets or has something, and that this judgement rests on a principle that is fundamental, binding, irrefutable, justified, established, accepted or the like, and also assert that it is not right and does not rest on such a principle that their only possible means of having the thing be used.

Can you, for example, assert someone's right to save his life in a certain situation, but not a right to the means? Can you assert a hungry child's right to good food in a situation and deny it the only means to food? Can you say it has a right to learn to read but no right to the only means to learning to read, say having a book? To repeat, can you assert someone's moral right to X and deny them the only possible means of getting X?

If the answer to that general question is no, then there is the upshot that so very many people who do accept the right of the Palestinians to a viable state but do not grant their right to the only means to that end are in contradiction. If they cannot bring themselves to give up the first claim of a right, to a state, they must also accept the second, to the necessary means to a state.

Further, if the only means to a viable state has in fact been terrorism, those who grant the right to a state must grant the right to the terrorism. As you will have gathered, that the Palestinians' only means to a viable state has been and may still be terrorism is something about which I myself have no doubt. Evidently it is a factual proposition in need of support. There was some of that in the sketch of the history of Palestine and Israel. There is enough there to lead me to think that the disinterested people who say the Palestinians had and have an alternative to terrorism are less moved by history and fact than by abhorrence for terrorism. The feeling cannot settle the question.

In any case, take it to be true at least for purposes of our reflection now that the Palestinians' only means to a viable state has been terrorism. That leaves us with the general question of whether granting a moral right to X entails granting a moral right to the only means to X? Each of these claims of a moral right, as you have heard, makes reference to a moral principle that is fundamental or the like.

It might be that the principle involved in the first claim is not the same principle involved in the second one. The first principle might be something about a people's freedom and power. The second might be about not taking innocent lives. When these principles conflict, as in the terrorism case, what is necessary is plainly a more fundamental and general principle, sometimes called an overriding or higher one. At any rate it will be one that adjudicates between the conflicting principles in the given case. For me and I hope you, the Principle of Humanity does this. But the present point is that *some* single principle is needed, indeed that reflection drives us to find one.

If that is so, there is a certain upshot. The fundamental principle applies to both the issue of the Palestinians' right to a viable state and the right to the only means to a viable state. Given this, there seems to be no possibility of according a moral right to a viable state but not a moral right to the means to it. You cannot do both. You surely cannot possibly get the opposed answers from the same principle. It will either be to the effect that the end is such that the only means must be accepted or that the only means are such that the right to the end cannot be accepted. Evidently, with respect to plain and clear talk about moral rights, and to take a simple example, I do not have a moral right to save my life by the only means that is the killing of three children.

My conclusion about Palestinian terrorism against neo-Zionist ethnic cleansing, a conclusion drawn before now in other writings and on other occasions, therefore remains for this and other reasons that, yes, this terrorism has been the moral right of the Palestinians. If this is a terrible conclusion, which it is, it seems to me also to be inescapable.

Understanding, Endorsing, Inciting

If you want to think about right and wrong with respect to Palestine, 9/11, Iraq, 7/7 and what will follow them, and if you first come to a general view of right and wrong, a view of what is decent, it will indeed have certain judgements as logical consequences. It will have these logical consequences, anyway, if you have got hold of something clear, a morality that is determinate, and if you can be confident about the facts of the situations. You don't have a choice about the consequences. It is not as if you can come to a confidence in the Principle of Humanity, and can see enough of the facts, and then it is up to you what is right.

To speak differently, if you are serious about right and wrong, which in fact is something that is in our natures as reason-users, you have to come to some summary of right and wrong. Anything else, any mixing of competing principles, values, virtues, insights, intuitions, feelings or whatever, will almost certainly be at least a kind of what Sartre called bad faith, a means of pretence. And it will not deal with the world you face, actually give you verdicts you need for action. In any case, the mixing *will* have a summary, whether or not you attend to it. Given the summary, and the facts of a situation, it is indeed true, isn't it, that you can't have it both ways when you are in trouble? You can't both step back from a judgement of justification and also hold on to the summary and the facts, can you? There isn't a third way for you, is there? You're not a politician in New Labour, are you?

The questions bring to mind a larger subject, which might be called the taxonomy or range of approvals and assents, and also Cherie Blair, a human rights lawyer and the wife of the British prime minister. A few years ago, in June 2002, as has been remembered often enough since, she attended an event in London at which an appeal for funds was launched by the charity Medical Aid for Palestinians. There was a presentation of graphic photos by a delegation just returned from Palestine. One of the delegation, Sir Andrew Green, chairman of the charity and former British ambassador to Saudi Arabia, said the situation of the Palestinians was shocking. For example, Palestinian towns were surrounded by Israeli barbed wire and ditches. Palestinians needing medical attention were kept waiting for hours at checkpoints by Israeli soldiers. He said that 'some Israelis themselves are now saying this amounts to a systematic oppression and humiliation of a people'.

The charity event took place some hours after a suicide bombing by a young Palestinian woman. Cherie Blair had something to say to journalists after the charity event:

> As long as young people feel they have got no hope but to blow themselves up, you are never going to make progress.

Her husband's office in Downing Street was put under pressure the next day by the effectively neo-Zionist newspaper the *Daily Telegraph* of Lord Conrad Black. She was presented as at least having shown sympathy with terrorism. The Israeli embassy in London attacked her comment, saying:

No political grievance or circumstance can justify the wilful targeting of civilians for political gain, nor can those who glorify and encourage such atrocities, teaching and preaching hatred and violence, be absolved of their responsibility for this terrible phenomenon.

In Jerusalem, a senior spokesman for the Israeli government said:

This is justification for terror. The suicide bombers are not doing it out of desperation. They are doing it because they are being cynically recruited with the promise of money and heaven.

Downing Street then made an apology for what had been said by the prime minister's wife. The prime minister himself said that hopes for the future in Palestine lay in the political process taking the place of the extremists, and that he was sure that was what his wife was saying.

What is the distance between arguing to the judgement that the Palestinians have had a moral right to their resistance to the taking of their land and Cherie Blair's saying that young Palestinians feel they have got no hope except to blow themselves up? The question is not perfectly simple. The Israeli embassy, as you have heard, effectively speculated that Cherie Blair was justifying the wilful targeting of civilians for political gain – justifying terrorism. The senior spokesman in Jerusalem declared that she was.

In fact the prime minister's wife was pretty clearly among those very many people who say they *understand* Palestinian terrorism. What do they mean? Do they mean no more than that they see *why* or *how* it has come about, as they might see why the door won't shut? Do they mean no more than what is meant by, say, a Jewish biographer of Hitler we can imagine, properly horrified by the Holocaust? He says that after considering Hitler's childhood, the development of his personality, pressures on him in the Nazi Party and various weaknesses in him, he the biographer now understands how it came about that Hitler carried forward his moral crime.

Evidently the many people may not mean just that kind of understanding. They may not be talking about bare or purely intellectual acceptance of or agreement with an explanation. They understand Palestinian terrorism in another of the dictionary senses of the word, where to understand some human action or practice is to be sympathetically aware of the nature or character of the action or practice. This *understanding* of a thing does fall short of *arguing and judging it to be right*, maybe a matter of a moral right. And, to persist for a while with the taxonomy or range of approval, it is clear that the latter asserting or expressing of an argument and opinion is different from *inciting* anyone to the action or practice in question.

The difference between arguing and judging something to be right and inciting someone to action directly or indirectly has long been established in and given value and honour to English and American law. English common law separates what is sometimes called *argued endorsement* or *reasoned argument* from incitement. Argued endorsement is what we have been much involved with – arguing something to be right, justifying it. Incitement is encouraging, inducing, inflaming, fomenting or indeed causing impassioned, emotional, unreflective or unthinking action by someone else. It is at least to share responsibility for his action. There is sense in the excess of saying that the action done is also the inciter's action.

English law recognizes a freedom to speak your mind or free speech that is not incitement. American law is stronger and goes further. Justice Learned Hand of the US Supreme Court affirmed the legal right to speak your mind so long as your words are not 'triggers to action'. Justice Felix Frankfurter affirmed that right even when you are advocating violence to bring about political change – presumably including a change of government. Justices Holmes and Brandeis distinguished advocacy from other speech that causes a 'clear and present danger'.

It is plain that argued endorsement, reasoned argument, justification, speaking your mind or speaking freely or putting a case in such a way *is* different from incitement, including actual incitement by glorification, exaltation or celebration – say by really intending to encourage or induce people to act by describing an act of terrorism in a certain circumstance in such a way that a listener would infer that he should emulate it. As John Stuart Mill said, there is a difference between expressing an opinion in a certain way, maybe in a newspaper, that corn-dealers are starvers of the poor, and declaring it to an excited mob before the house of a corn-dealer.

It would be innocent or foolish to deny that there are particular kinds of approval or assent that do not fall easily and clearly into either argued endorsement or free expression as against incitement. That is a wholly familiar truth about most differences and distinctions. It does not touch the main fact that there is a clear difference between almost all argued endorsement and almost all incitement. There remains a difference between endorsement and incitement despite the obvious truth, of which a low government may make use, that endorsement shades into incitement, that there is no *gap* between them, that in some cases it may be a decision rather than a discovery that separates two things. Endorsement and incitement remain as different as green from yellow, intentional from non-intentional, vehicles from non-vehicles, despite the fact that the greens shade into the yellows, the intentional into the non-intentional, and the vehicles into the non-vehicles. The fact of shading does not touch the main fact that there is a clear difference between almost all argued endorsement and almost all incitement.

Nor does the difference depend on law and lawyers and Mill. Remember that you can give your judgement that something is right, and indeed to be or to have been someone's right, where there can be no question whatever of exciting, stirring, impassioning or enraging the actor into action. There is the obvious case where the action judged is by someone dead, maybe in the distant past, and there is no significant and maybe no conceivable possibility of a repetition by somebody else. Further, you can say to someone that their doing something would be right and also their right, but that it definitely would not be in their self-interest – with the intended and comprehended meaning that they should not do it.

Another clear non-inciter, come to think of it, wrote a line in the

UN Declaration of Human Rights that you will remember about a people's right to rebellion against tyranny and oppression. There was the small extent of glorification in the line, by the way, that is open to a drafter of international law. The UN declaration is a little reminder, then, that while glorification and the like in certain circumstances can of course be incitement, there can be glorification, exaltation, celebration and what-not that definitely is not incitement.

Remember too all those governments, almost all of the United Nations, who by implication somehow supported but did not incite the Palestinians when they condemned neo-Zionism in their resolutions. Also various other non-inciters who have expounded parts of just war theory that have to do with what can be done against ethnic cleansing. They have included popes.

The whole matter of free expression is in fact misdescribed or weakly described as being about an individual's human, civil or other rights, by the way. It is in a way more important than this. What we all depend on is truth, factual truth above all but also moral truth. This is not only a commitment of the Principle of Humanity but the first necessity of life, the first necessity for our individual actions as well as our actions together. Often the truth does not announce itself. It needs help, usually against people who are against it. To deny truth the help of endorsement is to deny to ourselves what is fundamental to us. As Mill also maintained, there is an argument for the free expression of what is in fact false. To have it heard may make clearer and more forceful the opposite truth.

Can you still suppose that someone who comes or is driven to think that the Palestinians have had a right to their self-defence should say less or not speak out their judgement for some reason, perhaps say no more than that Palestinian self-defence is understandable? Should he or she give up the kind and degree of condemnation of neo-Zionism that is owed precisely to the assertion of a Palestinian right to kill in order to defeat it?

Or should he or she instead say what they believe? Should he or she run a risk, despite the precedents of English law, of attracting the attention of a government? A government that may be moved to action both by being disgraced for its part in a war elsewhere and apprehensive about terrorism at home and well able to make low use of the threat of it partly somehow to suggest they were right all along about something? A government that seeks to blur and makes vague the difference between reasoned endorsement and incitement, and pretends that some argued endorsement directed against that government is in fact what has hitherto for good reason been regarded as incitement? For a time after 7/7 that seemed possible in England despite honourable resistance from English judges and indeed the English law.

Well, you can come to believe in a principle and a morality, and it can issue not only in a conclusion about a moral right, as you have heard already, but in an obligation to state it, and to state it with all the force that truth allows. You can have an obligation to resist a government that threatens to widen the category of legal incitement beyond what is truly incitement and to subtract from the category of what is truly and rightly free speech. You can have an obligation to resist a government trying to run together glorification that is not incitement with glorification that is incitement.

You can have this obligation for more reasons than the great one having to do with the great value of argument and free expression. You can want, as I do, to keep the actual and good law on incitement effective because unconfused, and because you do not want ineffective and self-defeating steps to be taken against terrorism.

That is not all you should do in connection with neo-Zionism. You should take every rational step against it. You should not be quiet about the violation of the Palestinians because you are Jewish. You should get hold of Michael Neumann's book *The Case Against Israel*. You should support the simple solution to the simple Palestinian problem – the immediate and unnegotiated withdrawal of Israel from all of what remains to the Palestinians of their homeland. All of us should join those in the Church of England who want it to divest from the company that makes the caterpillar bulldozers that destroy the homes and lives of Palestinians. All of us should take part in all forms of boycott against retail stores and other businesses dealing with neo-Zionist Israel, civil disobedience, non-co-operation, not voting, picketing, ostracism, naming, symbolic public acts, strikes and whatever else is rational against neo-Zionism. We should see the need for a new disrespect, especially disrespect for a compliant political class. We should do what the New England Henry David Thoreau did in the nineteenth century, and not pay taxes to such a government as goes along with neo-Zionism.

We should not wait to disdain conventions exemplified by the one to the effect that a people on whose part terrorists act are never supported by that people. No one should have waited in their disdain until the democratic election of HAMAS in 2006 by the Palestinian people.

9/11

To be in one part of the world and to have been aware of it on 11 September 2001 was to remember it thereafter.

American Airlines Flight 11 carried 92 passengers and crew. It was flown by five Islamic suicide terrorists among the passengers into one of the twin towers of the World Trade Center in New York, symbols of American business. Another jet, United Airlines Flight 175, carried 65 passengers and crew. It was flown by more terrorists into the other tower. American Airlines Flight 77 with 64 people on board was crashed into the Pentagon, citadel of the American armed forces. A fourth airliner, United Airlines Flight 93, was being flown towards Washington and probably the White House. An order was given by the Vice President of the United States to the American Air Force to shoot it down. When some of the 44 passengers and crew attacked the cockpit, the plane was crashed by the terrorists into a field in Pennsylvania. The twin towers in New York, still burning, collapsed.

In all, about 2,800 persons were killed in the airliners, the towers and in the Pentagon, many horribly. Lives of many other people were made awful or worse.

That the actions of the killers were wrong was written on them.

To have an awareness of agony and destroyed lives, and to have a sense of the world as it was and its ordinary possibilities and probabilities, was and is to know that the actions were a hideous and monstrous wrong. This was and is known without need for much reflection on what might have been thought of or claimed by the killers or others as a consequence justifying their actions. To my mind, as you will gather, the wrong of 9/11 is to be taken as a kind of datum, a moral truth that has general moral principles as its possible consequences.

This is unaffected by something else, that there is certainly a question about the understanding of the wrong, a question about what made it the wrong it was. You can know a truth without knowing the reason for it.

Whatever is to be said about that, something else was and is as inescapable as the wrong of 9/11. It is that the killers themselves are to be held responsible for their actions. That is to say they are to be condemned for having done what they did when they could have done otherwise. It does not greatly matter whether we take their freedom to have consisted in free will, an originating of uncaused or undetermined decisions, or in voluntariness. If their freedom was of the latter kind, their actions were effects of those killers themselves, unconstrained by other people or other things, or by ignorance of the killers for which they were not at fault.

To hold them responsible for their actions, further, to condemn them for those actions, is to want to and to take what steps are now possible to reduce the possibility of more such actions. If we have backward-looking feelings of revulsion, of no relevance to the present and future, these are not what it mainly is for us to hold them responsible for their actions. To assign moral responsibility for a wrong is to see whose wrong it is, and thus usually to see who has to change or be changed. Since the 9/11 terrorists are dead, however, there is no more we can do in their connection than express our condemnation, in the hope and aim of reducing the chance of more such actions by others, reducing the chance of more of the same.

That we are right to hold the terrorists morally responsible, as I say, is surely as much a moral truth as that what they did was wrong. Indeed the two things are bound up together. The two judgements are, so to speak, two sides of one, on the thing done and on the doer. Admittedly, someone can do the wrong thing without moral responsibility if they are in fact ignorant of what it is that they are doing, or of the effects of what they are doing. A child can. This was in no sense the case with 9/11. There have been philosophers who have supposed, indeed in connection with terrorism and 9/11, that it is possible to know what one is doing, do the wrong thing, and not be held responsible for it. We need not agree, or linger over the matter.

As with the judgement on the wrongness of what was done, however, there is room for difference as to what makes our moral condemnation of the 9/11 terrorists what it is. The judgement can be engaged in unthinkingly. Different ideas of what it comes to can be had. Mistakes can be made. We need to avoid them.

The motivation of the 9/11 terrorists, like the motivation of other terrorists, has been the subject of question, speculation and conclusion, some by imaginative novelists. It has been supposed that they were in the grips of hatred of America. It has been supposed that they were evil. That is to say, presumably, that they were profoundly immoral and malevolent, perhaps in desiring the suffering of others for itself, taking the suffering as good in itself. It has been supposed that they were irrational, in one or all senses, or that they were mad or blinded by absurd and untrue religion.

How important is religion in Islamic or other terrorism? To my mind, as you may anticipate, it is about as important in itself as religion was conveyed to be in the sketch of the great human desires and goods in connection with the Principle of Humanity. Religion, you may remember, was given prominence in the goods of culture. But clearly the terrorism of which we now know has to do with all of the great goods, from decent lengths of life through to the goods of culture. It would in my view be wrong to suppose that Palestinian terrorism has as much to do with religion as with, say, freedom and power or respect and self-respect.

Admittedly the general matter of Islamic terrorism is complicated by the fact that the leaders of a people may be religious, and thus give a colouring to or indeed a vocabulary for the great human goods. So have other religious leaders, including our own. That does not turn freedom and power or respect and self-respect into other things than those that naturally have those names. Nor does the fact that a religion calls for lives of decent length not in pain make such lives first a part of religion or a matter of only religious importance.

The collection of thoughts and utterances about the motivation of the 9/11 terrorists contains the moral truths we have already, that their actions were hideous and monstrous in their wrong, and that they are to be held responsible for them. It also contains obscurity about hatred and evil. It contains forgetfulness about the use we ourselves have made of the suffering of others, and continue to make of it to this day. And thus forgetfulness of the need to consider purposes and more in the causing of suffering, and to think further of the standing of all those who cause suffering. The collection of thoughts and utterances on the motivation of the terrorists also contains nonsense if taken literally, as in the idea that the terrorists were insane, or merely in the grip of a hatred somehow without reason in it – good, bad or indifferent reason.

There would be no gain in our entering into all this dim stuff, much of it about 'anti-Americanism' as a puzzling prejudice or a somehow psychological condition, no gain in going beyond its large ingredient of the two moral truths. There is the reason for not entering into it that to do so is to support some of those in it already. Their aim or unconsidered impulse is to avoid or prevent a consideration of something it leaves out. That is more wrongs or possible wrongs than 9/11 in connection with 9/11.

It is notable that these partisans, and in particular Americans among them, do not have the support they might have expected from *The 9/11 Commission Report*, the official finding on the attacks prepared for the President, the United States Congress, and the American people. If it does not dwell on possible wrongs, or take a final view of them, it does not overlook them either. Nor does the report support other nonsense.

There is another matter. It is a familiar fact that there can be *shared* moral responsibility for an action, policy or the like and its consequences. The action or whatever can be owed to more than one person. More persons than the final actor or actors can be held morally responsible or credited with moral responsibility – disapproved of or approved of in some degree, for contributing to the action and its consequences. They have done wrong in providing certain of the necessary conditions of the final action. Knowing what they were doing, or not knowing when they should have known, they have done something such that if they had not done it, the final wrong action would not have happened. Further, they have done wrong in making a contribution of a certain size.

Moral responsibility is in this respect the same as legal responsibility. To be one of a number of participants in a murder, to hire someone to torment a lawful tenant out of a house, to incite someone to injure someone, or to bribe someone about a contract, is to have a certain part of the legal responsibility. There is a host of such possibilities in the law. You can be one of the offenders or be partly responsible on account of negligence, or because you made something possible or probable. You can be partly responsible because of an omission as distinct from a positive act. A judge may in fact quantify the contributions of several or more persons with respect to something. Someone may be held legally responsible for 36 per cent of a loss.

We need to ask if there were certain necessary conditions of 9/11 that require us to include more than the terrorists in considering the question of moral responsibility for 9/11. This does not much depend on the subsequent explanation of the attacks by Osama bin Laden and others. The explanation had in it Palestine, the effects of a UN embargo on Iraq and particularly on Iraqi children after the first Iraq war in 1990, and what was asserted to be the desecration by America of the religion of Islam and the culture of the Muslims in Saudi Arabia and elsewhere. It is indeed plain to anyone half in

touch with recent history, without help from bin Laden, that in considering the general question of moral responsibility for 9/11 we
have to ask about Palestine.

We have to consider the fact of neo-Zionism, the expansion of
Israel beyond its original borders, with the consequences of this for
the Palestinian people. We will make up our own minds, but we
cannot conceivably leave out of consideration what the world
believes. This, to give a cautious report of it that cannot be doubted,
is that 9/11 would not have happened without the fact of neo-
Zionism with its consequences, and that a question arises about the
right or wrong of neo-Zionism. A question arises, that is, about the
role in 9/11 of some other terrorism than that of 9/11, the right or
wrong of it. A question arises about the terrorism of neo-Zionism.

There can be no scintilla of doubt that neo-Zionism *has* been
terrorism as we have understood it, understood it in a standard way.
If its illegality is owed to a recent history of international law in
which people as well as national states have come to have rights, that
is no troublesome fact. We have learned a little. But do you now
want to pause in our inquiry into the possibility of shared responsibility for 9/11? Do you want to call a halt, reopen a question, as
perhaps you did once before, and then introduce and proceed by
way of another definition of terrorism – now that neo-Zionism falls
together with the atrocity of 9/11?

You will need to ask yourself why. You will need to give us a
reason. Your new definition, further, to think of one possibility, will
not be able to depend on the horror of 9/11 to make only it into terrorism. There has been horror in the killings of neo-Zionism, some
of it in refugee camps. Nor will your new definition serve much
purpose if it limits terrorism, consistently, to what is done officially
as against unofficially, to what is done by other than the officers or
uniformed officers of states, maybe in charge of concentration
camps. Something that is no longer called terrorism may remain
exactly a culpable necessary condition of such a wrong as 9/11, a
necessary condition, just as vicious as before, just as much a wrong
itself.

We are serious here. If there is sense in our definition and balance, we are not reasoning by association, not reasoning by putting a name on a thing. It is the things that matter, their nature, not which aspect of them we use in order to identify them.

To add up the questions we need to ask about 9/11, they are as follows. What made it the wrong it was? Are others than the 9/11 terrorists themselves to be held responsible for it? Was it also their wrong? Are neo-Zionists to be condemned for 9/11? Are those of us who support them, perhaps by omission, also to be held responsible? Are Americans in particular, above all their leaders, but also most of their intellectuals, to be morally judged for the attacks on 9/11 against themselves? Are those leaders, and those who have most power in putting them in place, to be judged for killings of their own citizens?

Think back on conceivable means of answering these questions, certain bodies of thought and certain practices. Think back on democracy. Suppose for a moment the wrong of 9/11 had at least much to do with its being an attack on democracy, on the great instantiation of democracy as we have it, the United States. If so, you are on the way to the upshot that America has no responsibility whatever for 9/11.

This is because American support of neo-Zionism, like neo-Zionism itself, is and has been democratic in our ordinary understanding of democracy. There is no possibility of holding persons or people responsible for something by way of a prior action or policy that in fact was not wrong – as it would not be if democracy was the test of right. I avoid spending more time on complexities here by asking one question.

But *was* 9/11 wrong because it was an attack on a democracy? Of course not. To escape for an instant from the dismal convention owed to most of our politicians and their makers and their thinkers is to know that 9/11 would indeed have been the monstrous thing it was if America had not been the hierarchic democracy it was. Would ordinary people not have been burned alive or leapt from the two towers if America was something other than a hierarchic democracy, ruled differently? Whatever is to be said of innocence, would fewer than 2,800 somehow innocent persons be dead if America did not have an elected president? Would there have been no horror, or much less, if an American army general was resident in the White House?

9/11 patently was not wrong because it was an attack on a democracy. Rather, 9/11 gave support to the view that what makes things right or wrong in our world is something else. What makes things wrong is that they make for bad lives, sometimes unspeakably bad lives. What made 9/11 wrong was what we all know, that it ended 2,800 lives, ended personal worlds, and took most of the value from many others. The actions of the terrorists were wrong because with certainty they ended and affected many lives horribly without any conceivable confidence of a greater good.

It was certain that the attacks would do what they immediately did. In contrast, it was worse than uncertain, a dream of rage and passion, that they would achieve or contribute to a goal, in particular the goal of the Principle of Humanity. The attacks could work in just the other way. They could have horrendous results, maybe war. Maybe war against Iran or Iraq. Whatever you may think of Hiroshima, 9/11 was not Hiroshima. Whatever you think of our terror bombing of Dresden, 9/11 was not Dresden.

You will excuse me, I think, from a further consideration of the other possible ways of thinking of wrong and right and thereby of shares of moral responsibility in connection with 9/11. Do return yourself if you want to those incomplete helps or makeshifts or worse – from reliance on only negotiation to conservatism and liberalism. For reasons of which you knew before we came to terrorism, some of them having to do with our human nature, and now for the further reason of 9/11 itself, we will proceed on the basis of the Principle of Humanity, that principle on which humanity converges.

It is what explains the wrong of 9/11 itself. It is what explains the responsibility had by the terrorists on the airplanes. To come to an answer to a question we were contemplating, the principle and certain facts are what makes other necessary conditions of 9/11 wrong and hence *do* give a share of moral responsibility to the people in question. The people in question with 9/11 are indeed neo-Zionists, as real as the people on the airplanes. Some of them are Americans. A wrong done to Americans, 9/11, was partly brought about by a wrong done by these Americans. 9/11 itself was partly a wrong of Americans. Other Americans, and others than Americans, have also been morally at fault for tolerating the violation of the Palestinian homeland and the Palestinians.

I also take it that you will excuse my passing by a desire of neo-Zionists and their sympathizers to pretend that neo-Zionism was not a necessary condition of 9/11 at all. That 9/11 did not happen first of all because of neo-Zionism. This is pretence, mainly conscious pretence.

That 9/11 would not have happened without neo-Zionism and what flowed from it is on the way to being as indubitable as that Louis XIV and the *ancien régime* were a necessary condition of the French Revolution. It is of course imaginable or conceivable without self-contradiction that the attack would have happened in a different world without neo-Zionism and the passion and history it has engendered, but no practical realism in judgement spends time on the piece of imagination. Nor does time need to be spent on the idea that to assign to neo-Zionism a real share of responsibility for 9/11 is to suppose absurdly that it was sufficient to produce 9/11 by itself, that it was a complete causal circumstance for the event.

There is another conclusion about parts in 9/11, shared responsibility. It is not much less important. You can think it is more important. I do.

It is often the case, with the wrong done by final actors, that it also has what is at least arguably a necessary condition of relevance in something other than an earlier action by others of the sort we have had in mind. There is something other than an action commonly taken to be what you might call a *most immediate* necessary condition of the final wrong. In connection with 9/11, there is something different from neo-Zionism and support for it, and also such other possible sources of responsibility as the embargo on Iraq and the claimed desecration of Muslim religion and culture.

Think for a moment of the analogy of ordinary punishment by the state of ordinary criminals. Think of two earlier offences, perhaps being part of a plot, that make for a share of responsibility for a later one. One earlier offence is by a man otherwise exemplary, with no criminal record. One is by a man known for other earlier offences, an offender of known viciousness. The first offender, as we may say, must be taken as someone to be usefully reasoned with, someone open to kinds of appeal, someone to be punished only in a certain way. The second is otherwise. He gets a different sentence.

Return to morality and contemplate conceivable wrongs by the doers of earlier actions. It may well be true that earlier additional wrongs, although not most immediate, *are* also relevant necessary conditions of the later wrong. To speak of the fact in question differently, an earlier action may be in a *context* of actions, and that context may be as necessary a condition as a most immediate earlier action. It may be an enabling context. It is therefore the case that others than the final doers may be held responsible for the terrorism in a way additional to the one we have already.

In connection with 9/11, you can put aside Palestine, Iraqi children and so on for a time, and usefully spend a little time with Africa. You can spend a little time with African demography, and more particularly average lifetimes – average lengths of life in societies. Also the history of changes in average lifetimes of various of our own societies, where dramatic increases have been brought about.

If you spend the time with African figures that were available in 2001, you will find out a certain thing mentioned in passing earlier about the poorest tenths of population in the poor African countries of Malawi, Mozambique, Sierra Leone and Zambia. You will conclude, given what America, Britain and the rich North of the world in general could have done for them, that those persons now alive in the poorest tenths are being deprived of twenty million years of living time. If you use figures available in 2005, the loss of living time is greater.

We treat them like animals, or lower animals.

The day of 11 September 2001 can come to mind in a different way. On it, 2,800 persons lost their lives in the four airliners, the twin towers, and the Pentagon. On that day, too, if deaths by starvation were spread evenly throughout the year, 24,000 people starved to death.

Do you say now that I am blaming 9/11 on American omissions with respect to Africa? I am not, unless you are using words in a surprising way. What seems to me to need saying is that additions can be and must be made to the moral responsibilities of the nineteen Islamic terrorists for 9/11. It is not only they whose wrong it was, not only their possible successors who have to change or be changed. We have to add in a share of responsibility for neo-Zionism itself. We have to add in our share, particularly our leaders' share, for tolerating neo-Zionism. We have to add in a share on account of a context for our toleration, what else we do and fail to do. In that context there is the depriving of people now alive of the twenty million years.

We can also think about shares of responsibility having to do with more context – denials of others of the great goods than a decent length of life. But leave that.

9/11 and a Troubling Question

You will not suppose that that is the end of what needs thinking and saying about 9/11, here and elsewhere. You will want to add a good deal about the moral responsibility of bin Laden and others for the hell of that day. To this I have not the slightest resistance. There can be little hesitation about assigning to him more responsibility than to the nineteen terrorists on the airliners. Leaders do more. The actions of leaders multiply actions by others. My concern has been with other leaders, leaders in our world, for the reason not of their greater responsibility but for the reason that they are more our responsibility.

You may not have failed to take in that what has been said makes it possible to raise a question about the intended consequences of those who brought about the hell of 9/11. The question, not to avoid it, is whether the killings and the rest, from the point of view of the Principle of Humanity, would have been right under certain circumstances that did not at all obtain. Would they have been right *if* it could have been well judged in advance that they were a rational means, an effective means worth paying, to the end of the Principle of Humanity?

That the question is likely to be raised by someone disinclined to the principle or the use of it does not make the question pointless. Certainly there is reason to look for what may have the force of counter-examples to a moral principle, consequences in imagined and unreal situations but consequences that seem or are unacceptable and put in question or defeat the principle. We cannot ignore the question of whether the killings have been right if our world was not as it was, and did not have in it just the possibilities and probabilities of which we know.

We have not given serious attention to all the possible or conceivable consequences in the minds of the men on the airliners and the men and women behind them or on their side. We have, for reason enough, concentrated on a possible or conceivable consequence connected to certain of our own responsibilities. That is the possible consequence that is the ending of support of whatever kind for neo-Zionism. To this has been added the possible consequence that is an improvement in a world of starvation and the like.

Suppose we were to press on, as we shall not, to what would seem to be the best informed and best judged view of what rationally could have been anticipated in terms of consequences of 9/11 – other than those immediate and hellish consequences of death and agony in New York, Washington and Pennsylvania. Suppose, that is, that we were to arrive at a good view of the non-hellish consequences, a certain state of affairs, that could have been anticipated as the consequences of the means that was 9/11 – the means of the first hellish consequences.

We could then frame a first question. It would be the question of whether that state of affairs, taken in itself, without reference to means to it, would be preferable to other states of affairs, without reference to means to them, from the point of view of the Principle of Humanity. I have no hope of satisfying myself quickly as to a guess about that, let alone satisfying you.

There would also be the question of whether the means of 9/11, if it could be known in advance that they would issue in the non-hellish state of affairs, would have the support of the Principle of Humanity. The question can reasonably be asked. It can as reasonably be said in reply that it cannot be answered. An answer would require, for a start, an answer to the prior question, that of what is in a certain state of affairs, and the question of whether it would be preferable to others in terms of humanity.

If you now anticipate at least uneasiness from me, about a principle and a morality, you face disappointment.

That these questions trouble or defeat us does not begin to entail uncertainty about the answer to the question of whether 9/11 was wrong in terms of humanity. It was. Nor is there uncertainty about the answers to the other questions, about responsibility. The same will be true of any like atrocities. Nor does the existence of these questions show some weakness or vulnerability of the morality in question. There are *no* serious moralities, no moralities that pass some initial test of reflection or get the consideration of decently critical judges, that do not face questions of a defeating or paralysing kind.

You heard some way back of Kant's deontological declaration that giving criminals what they deserve is an absolute obligation on us. Really? Although human life were made intolerable? *All* human life? Other animals too? Who actually believes that justice is to be done although the heavens really do fall? Although the result is any torment that can be described? No one to whom we need to pay attention believes this. And if a moralist performs some marriage between a principle about good consequences and a principle really of another kind, supposing there to be such a thing, it will take hardly longer to devise a terrible question.

Morality can be easier than questions of fact and yet defeating. I can make no claim of completeness in defence of the Principle of Humanity. Nor can you, very likely, if you depart from it in favour of anything else. Did you think life was easy? Did you think thinking about life was easy? Maybe you don't read a decent paper or turn on television that carries information. Maybe you have not had that thought that a complete and untroubled morality must be a mistake. Life is harder than that.

One other subject is more tractable. What ought our response to 9/11 have been? An answer does not depend on our having what we have not got, a satisfactory account of intended consequences of the attack other than the hellish ones. One of those intended consequences, the first mentioned and the most salient, was our ceasing to support neo-Zionism. As you will anticipate from what you have heard already, it seems to me indubitable that this would have been right. So too would it have been right to act with respect to the losing, now, of the twenty million years. Both things would be right now, as you read these words.

Do you say a further response to 9/11, not at all an intended consequence of it, was also right – the taking of all possible steps to prevent more such terrorism? That is as true. *Certainly* that is as true. It was right for us to set out to prevent further horrors by security measures and indeed something or other that might indeed be called a war on terrorism, in fact on some terrorism in particular. Should we also have gone to war – war on a country?

Is it somehow pointless to make the first judgement? Is it pointless to direct attention to causes of terrorism that we have an obligation to try to end, such causes as neo-Zionism? Well, you can't pick up a half-decent newspaper without reading something like that, however emollient. But you may have the view that because of the want of urgency in the newspapers, the calm of them, we will not be awakened from a sleep of self-interest, that 9/11 could not do that and nothing will. Still, it is not a sleep of self-interest, but just of supposed self-interest. It is not all of us in our societies of the West and North, or most of us, who benefit from the way things are.

The mistake may catch our attention when we have a moment of wakefulness.

Iraq

There was more than 9/11 in the past of the almost entirely American and British war on Iraq or at any rate on Iraqis that began in March 2003.

Saddam Hussein had carried forward Iraq's history of autocracy, hostility and conflict – monarchy, nationalist agitation and repression, coups, military government, purges and treason trials. This history was owed in part, after the collapse of the Ottoman Empire in World War 1, to the fact of the British protectorate under the mandate of the League of Nations. This late imperialism forced together territories of the Shia and the Sunni Muslims and also the Kurds, mainly for the benefit of the protector.

Saddam Hussein came to power officially in 1979, having killed some hundreds of political opponents. He had the ambition of leading the Arab world against the West and Israel, and continued to rule by repression and persecution, much of it carried out by security police. As the president of the United States noted later, he made use of torture in his jails, notably Abu Ghraib in Baghdad. He also used poison gas to continue Iraq's suppression of the Kurds in the north of the country, killing more than 5,000 in the town of Halabja, for which he was especially remembered thereafter. In fact about 500,000 Kurds seeking independence had been killed, mainly by Iraq and Turkey, since 1923.

In the Iraq–Iran war of 1980–88, said to be about a waterway, the United States favoured Iraq, having given it a green light for the war and to some extent armed it. Dual-use technology was supplied that could be used to make chemical and biological weapons. Allegedly gas was used by both sides in the war, during which one million lives were lost. To the United States, Iraq was preferable to the radical

Islamic Iran of the ayatollahs, which had showed its revolutionary zeal and unpredictability by holding 52 Americans hostage in Tehran. The war also carried a possible threat to America of Iran coming to control the oil in Kuwait and Saudi Arabia. Israel's bombing of an Iraqi nuclear reactor in 1981, in extraordinary defiance of international law, added to Iraqi hostility to Zionism and neo-Zionism.

Kuwait was a creation of the British and French after World War 1, and was thereafter a kind of estate of an installed royal family, the Sabahs. With some reason it had long been claimed as a province by Iraq. Saddam's 1990 invasion and attempted annexation of it was also owed to a dispute about oil revenues. He may have thought, as a result of a careless American communication, that he had got another green light. The invasion resulted in the defeat of Iraq by an international alliance led by the United States and Britain. About 13,000 civilians were killed by American and allied forces, and about 70,000 died later from war-related causes. During the war, Iraq launched missiles against Israel.

This 1990 war and the conditions of the peace treaty were followed by United Nations arms inspections and prolonged international trade sanctions against Iraq. These were a persistent attempt to prevent the regime's having or coming to have chemical, biological and nuclear weapons – such weapons of mass destruction as were already possessed by Israel. Some or all of Iraq's chemical weapons were destroyed, as was a nuclear project. Saddam Hussein's regime was not fully co-operative, taking the view that the inspections were concealing American and in effect Israeli espionage against Iraq. This had to be admitted in part subsequently.

The sanctions were in at least one way effective. The UN reported in 1997 that deaths due to hunger or lack of medicines owed to the sanctions exceeded one million. Of these, 570,000 were of children. There were also American and British air raids against military targets from 1998 to 2003, and continued threats of war.

The first large American response to the terrorism against it of 11 September 2001, however, was not the war on Iraq that began in

March 2003, but a previous one worth noting, partly for reasons of comparison. The first response was the attack in Afghanistan on the radical fundamentalist Muslim movement, the Taliban. It had won control of the country, partly by the use of American arms supplied to it earlier for its struggle against the Russians. The Taliban, having refused to hand over Osama bin Laden, at least the inspiration of 9/11, paid the price. Also, American bombs and missiles caused over 3,000 civilian deaths, many of them horrible.

As you have heard, it has been my view, shared with so many, that our immediate response to 9/11 ought to have been both to fight Islamic terrorism and to fight the causes of Islamic terrorism, causes for which we have had a responsibility, causes that were wrongs done by us.

You can try to argue that the attack on the Taliban with the civilian deaths, the collateral damage, was defensible on grounds of which you know, at bottom the Principle of Humanity. To that justification of the attack can be added, so far as it can be added consistently, that a country subjected to an atrocity of the kind of 9/11 has less choice open to it than may be supposed. Human nature exists. A fact of it not mentioned so far is that it puts limits on our reactions to such horrors as 9/11. What we have little choice but to do, having been attacked, is not all that would be right if we were not so human. Not all too human. 'Ought' implies 'can' in more than simple ways. So does 'ought to refrain' imply 'can refrain'.

As for dealing not with Islamic terrorism itself, but with the causes of it, including suffering, distress and deprivation, we did nothing. None of the articles by thoughtful Americans in the *International Herald Tribune* about addressing the matter of Palestine, or any related wrong, had any significant effect whatever. In Britain, Blair's speeches were only Blair's speeches.

The forces that invaded Iraq after March 2003 consisted in about 135,000 Americans and about 45,000 British. They were accompanied by token contingents from other countries – including 3,000 men from Italy, 2,000 from Australia, and 900 from Spain. There were a few personnel or gestures of help from about 25 other countries as a result of strenuous invitations from the United States. France, Germany, Russia and most of the world declined them.

Now as these words are written in 2006, the bloody occupation that followed on the war continues. There are ongoing killings by insurgents of Americans and those taken as collaborating with them. People die every day, sometimes by the dozen. More than 2000 American soldiers have been killed. As remarked earlier, about 60,000 Iraqi civilians have been killed, the possible count of them by the occupiers not made or kept secret. Those crippled or maimed are far more numerous. Presumably there is less torture and sexual violation of prisoners by Americans in the Baghdad prison than before it leaked out. The democratic Iraqi government denies that it does very much of the same torturing that was done by Saddam. If some or many Iraqis wanted liberation from him, they don't want what they have got. The pretence that resistance consists mainly in other Arabs than Iraqis has been given up.

Was our starting of the war right or wrong? Has its continuation since May 2003, when Bush in effect announced that it was over, been right or wrong? In my view, as you know, the answers to these questions must come from the morality of the Principle of Humanity. As in the case of answers given to questions about Palestine, they will also depend on judgements of fact, perhaps less disputable judgements of fact. In sum, was going to war and keeping at it, on the best available judgement and knowledge, the rational means to the end of getting or keeping people out of bad lives, Iraqis in particular. Was that the probable outcome of invasion and occupation?

A way of coming to and organizing or setting out an answer to the question is firstly by way of given and other reasons for our embarking on and continuing the war, and secondly by way of reflection on those reasons.

Firstly, what were the reasons or intentions or whatever that moved our leaders and their supporters, whether announced or unannounced reasons, whether correct or incorrect anticipations of consequences? To see them, as always, was to be able to form a judgement of what would happen in the war and after it. Also, relatedly, what was the effectiveness, weight or strength of the various considerations in the thinking and feeling of our leaders? What size of contribution would particular reasons make to what would happen? To answer the question was also to be able better to judge what would actually happen in the war and after it.

Secondly, to come to the reflection on the reasons, were the given and ungiven ones good or bad? Could they add up to a consideration of consequences that justified war?

There was much loose talk about why we were attacking Iraq. Much of it assumed, like our leaders, that the full explanation was simple. But hardly any full explanation is simple. Think of a causal circumstance for any large human endeavour or policy that in turn has many effects, diverse effects. It is as good as certain that the causal circumstance itself will have in it many elements. In fact there is some kind of truth about causation there. The complex is not produced by the simple.

In America, Bush said that America and the world were in imminent danger of attack by horrible weapons of mass destruction. We in Britain were told by Blair that we were going to war to defend ourselves against the possibility or probability of imminent attack. Blair said we could be attacked by existing weapons of mass destruction 45 minutes after the order was given by Saddam Hussein. Rarely has a national danger been declared to be more clear and present by a head of state. Never, perhaps, has it been so gravely affirmed that an attack by us would be pre-emptive self-defence. It was crucial that the dictator, unlike the democrat, could not be trusted to tell the truth about things, above all about his weapons of mass destruction. *He* had some record of deception. *He* would lie.

Perhaps this reason or explanation of our going to war, attack in 45 minutes, is better described in another way. It was that our leader and those around him were aware that he would be allowed to make use of what his fellow-citizens did not really or fully believe. They would in effect defer to their elected prime minister. They would go along with him despite at least an uncertainty as to literal truth. He had a convention on his side. Still, here was a reason for war.

A second reason given was that we needed to go to war against Islamic terrorism in general. We needed to go to war to reduce the probability of more of this terrorism. The American president connected Iraq with 9/11. He allowed half of his countrymen to suppose the attack of 9/11 was somehow the work of Saddam Hussein in person. This he did by the juxtaposition of paragraphs in speeches and the useful proposition that Saddam Hussein and Osama bin Laden were both enemies of America.

It is likely that in fact the president had grasped from his advisers that Iraq and what was called al-Qaeda were not at all bedfellows, that Iraq under Saddam Hussein was precisely not a nation of religious radicalism. What the president and others were engaged in, being unable to find bin Laden, was choosing the best available target, however relevant, in order to convey threat, determination and the like to all the targets unavailable to them. The war on Iraq, in part, was plainly a war *pour encourager les autres*.

Something else, already alluded to, was not precisely a third reason for going to war, but a kind of excuse, more implied than stated. This was a smaller fact related to the fact about the Taliban and Afghanistan – that human nature and a nation's nature are such that there are certain impossibilities, or anyway near-impossibilities. If we had a choice about Iraq, it was nonetheless the case that we were subject to a kind of necessity, compulsion or constraint. We could not let affronts to us and the world go without reply. In particular we could not but take action against a barbaric regime not quickly complying with what we said to be international law, not quickly complying with resolutions of the United Nations, requirements laid down by civilization.

We were told more explicitly, although belatedly, after doubts arose about Iraqi weapons of mass destruction, that there was the clear reason for going to war that we would be toppling a vile dictator, saving his people from him. He had used chemical weapons on his own people, these being those unfortunates included in Iraq who were Kurds. He could do worse, cause more suffering. This was a humanitarian intervention on our part. This was what international conscience required. This was not about oil, as the American vice-president in particular declared finally and for ever.

Also, this was not only a war against an evil man and somehow evil itself, but a war for democracy and by democracies. We would bring democracy to Iraq, the freedom and equality of it. That was our mission. Further, we would in our attack have the particular confidence of which you have heard. We would have the confidence of being in the right that attaches to democracies when they are in disagreement or conflict with a non-democracy.

These five considerations already added up to something else. War would take lives. American and British soldiers, if not very many, would lose their lives. But this, we were given to understand, would be a case where the end would justify the means. A price would have to be paid for safeguarding ourselves from immediate attack, reducing the probability of more Islamic terrorism generally, acting on a kind of necessity of nature, bringing down a monster, and giving democracy to a people. But it would be a price worth paying.

There were yet more considerations. One was the proposition that the war would be legal, according to international law. It would have been worthwhile getting a UN resolution actually permitting the war for reasons having to do with Iraqi weapons of mass destruction. But there already was a perfectly adequate resolution. It required suitable interpretation, but we could have the assurance of our government law officer in his independence of his leader and of politics that it was entirely sufficient. As in the case of the 45-minute danger, there is also a more realistic version of this reason for war. It was, simply, that the government could pretend legality and be known to pretend it without paying much of a price.

In Britain we all knew that something else was also moving our British leader and those around him. This seventh thing was alliance with America. The alliance had in it politics of reality. It was in our national interest to be less independent of America than the French, the Germans and the rest of the world, who took the war to be at least illegal. We had more reason than, say, the Spanish Prime Minister José María Aznar. Our alliance also had in it a shared history and language. We had fought other wars together. There was also something to be discerned more important than the shared history and language and at least as important as the politics of reality. In fact it stands by itself as part of what took us to war.

This factor was an ideology. It was an ideology shared by Bush, Blair, Cheney, most of the New Labour Party and all of the American administration. Most of the British government and almost all of the American government were within and subject to the political tradition of conservativism, a tradition open to analysis and evidently serving the self-interest not of a nation but of part of a nation. It now had privatization in it, the buying and selling of even more of life, with the main profit to a part of a society. You heard something of this tradition earlier, along with the tradition of liberalism, and then a little more of it in connection with our hierarchic or primitive democracy and what was called the consortium.

Do you perhaps say that this idea about ideology as among the causes of a war is imagination, maybe akin to conspiracy theory? That the war against Iraq has had nothing much to do with ideology? That to put it forward as part of the explanation of a war is the weightless speculation of a philosopher, maybe a philosopher too attracted to and too impressed by ideas?

Well, consider for a start whether in this circumstance it would have been likely, as likely, that Britain's New Labour Party would readily have become an essential ally of a nation of a significantly different ideology. Would we have responded well to a government not so like ours in seeing the reality of the world, the imperatives clear to those who have made their way in the real world and also made money? Would we have stood so firmly with a government not informed by an orderly and proper religion, an understanding of the natural way with respect to societies, a good sense of the problems of the ideal of equality? What about standing so firmly with the insufficiently reformed or perhaps too reformed government of Russia? I take it that you are pretty sure that we would not so readily have lined up with Cuba in the possible world where our interests in other ways fell in with those of Fidel Castro?

Bush and his supporters and Blair and New Labour did indeed see a war as an assertion of the rational, the realistic and the proven over more or less the opposite, a darkness, extremism and fanaticism, and indeed evil incarnate and otherwise. That in effect they said so is not what the proposition depends on. Who, on reflection, can doubt it?

Something else can be separated not only from ideology but also from alliance and the politics of reality. This was a conviction as to the interest of America, Britain and friends in terms of exactly oil, such corporations as the American vice-president's old one, and so on. Occasional economists and maybe more journalists specializing in economics have informed us that Iraq was *all* about the world's oil resources in Iraq and in the Middle East generally and the petro-dollar. That cannot be true. No doubt it is a very considerable part of the truth.

That ninth item is not the end of the elements in a decent explanation of our going to war against Iraq. One, the second last, is larger than at least some of those above.

All of us who read a decent newspaper in either America or Britain knew too that another thing taking us to war was more particular than the political tradition of conservatism, although somewhat adventitiously connected with it. That was what was called neo-conservatism in Washington. The principal part of this thinking and feeling, or a part as principal as any other, had to do with Palestine. Certainly neo-conservatism was somehow supportive of Israel, a continuation of the opposition noted several times in the brief history of Iraq with which we began. It was a matter of some Jewish Americans and some other Americans with divided or dual loyalties.

There is a further question about this support, the nature of neo-conservatism. Was it Zionism or neo-Zionism? Well, there is a fact that might have been remarked on before now, and needs to be remembered in other connections than the present one. It is that there is a big difference between Zionism and neo-Zionism. I do not mean to add something to one of their definitions, which you will remember, but rather to remind you that the first, Zionism, has actually been achieved.

Taken as the project of the founding and security of Israel in its original borders, 80 per cent of Palestine, Zionism is a fact. It is a notably settled and secure fact, about as much so as most such national facts. There is well-known pretence to the contrary by neo-Zionism, of course. But a nuclear power, a military power greater than all others but three in the world, a nation guaranteed by the world's only superpower, is not about to be driven into the sea, whatever ritualistic threats may be heard from a speechifying head of another state. Any other idea, founded on whatever ritual speech or document, is absurd illusion or culpable abuse of truth.

It follows, if any argument is needed, that an indubitable element in the explanation of the war against Iraq, neo-conservative support of Israel, was precisely neo-Zionism. It seems there is a general truth here. In general, if a question arises about the aim and purpose of support of any kind for Israel now, the question has a certain answer. The aim and purpose can hardly be for what exists and in fact is under no threat and is not insecure.

Finally, there was the element in the explanation of the war that was the personal motivation of our leaders, often said to be their desires to secure their places in history. What went with this was the satisfactions, self-esteem and the excitement of more members of what it is reasonable enough to call the political class. It has an interest that it defends, a power whose exercise satisfies it.

It is not true, as I read on a university wall, that all politicians are shits. A few exceptions who come to my mind at the moment are Benn, Cook, Dalyell, Foot, Galloway, Gilmour, Hattersley, Jefferson, Mullin, Adlai Stevenson, maybe Clinton, and Profumo, the last of whom had the distinction not only of resigning office for having lied but of then removing himself from the scene. Their honourable existence does not put in question the natures of so many around them.

Iraq Conclusions,
Killing Innocents

We have assembled reasons or intentions with respect to war on Iraq, spoken or unspoken. They include anticipations of consequences and the like that were taken by our leaders and their supporters as justifying the war or useable in pretence of justification. Let us look through them, in the order in which they were set out. Let us try to see what would have been the best possible judgement on these reasons and supposed reasons for war, these anticipated or pretended consequences of starting and continuing the war, as distinct from the judgement of our leaders.

To begin not with the first item on the list, but with the bit of history of Iraq under Saddam, it is a grim story. It is not overwhelmingly different, however, either from what preceded it in Iraq or what has taken place under other dictatorships, military governments and the like. Indeed it is not even much different. Saddam Hussein added very little to the terrible history of the Kurds. He added less than our uninvaded ally, Turkey. In fact he added greatly less than us.

But the principal point about this history is that we were fully implicated in almost all of it, despite the conflict over Kuwait. We were not at all involved in rescuing a people from vicious leaders. Our contribution to Saddam's own career was considerable. So was our contribution to the deaths of 500,000 Iraqi children.

These considerations at the very least put in serious doubt the idea that war on Iraq was importantly a humanitarian intervention. They raised the question of whether selective humanitarianism is humanitarianism. You could not expect, in 2003 or thereafter, given the history, and if you looked over other reasons for war, that the consequences of American and British action would in fact go far to fulfil the official aims of the United Nations, the Red Cross, or Amnesty International. You would not expect them to go far in serving the end of the Principle of Humanity.

The most salient of the purported reasons for war was the first one, pre-emptive defence of America and Britain against possible immediate attack. Blair and Bush lied or else indulged in self-deception as vicious, half-conscious self-deception. They were close to suborning less compliant parts of their intelligence services in order to secure useful judgements of danger, which they then manipulated and falsified.

No one properly sceptical had to wait for the mounting evidence, the accumulation of it ending in flat proof, to see that there was no reason whatever for war in the proposition that it was needed to save us from imminent attack by weapons of mass destruction. Indeed, it took something close to a fool actually to believe that Saddam Hussein, clearly no fool himself, and no mad idealist and no martyr, would take such a suicidal course. That America and Israel are nuclear powers is not some fantasy of their detractors.

In fact Bush is not only the president of whom the car-bumper sticker says that some village in Texas has lost its idiot. Blair is not just a salesman of social panaceas who has educated himself only in the law. Both had some grip on the actual probabilities as to Iraqi weapons of mass destruction. They knew that imminent attack was nonsense. The importance of this fact is not in the judgement of their moral personalities in themselves. One impor-tance is that it could be judged in 2003 that they could not be trusted as to *any* probable consequences of the war in general – consequences, after all, over which they would have continuing control or influence.

What of the idea that a second reason for war was to reduce Islamic terrorism in general? In fact it was a very good judgement in 2003 and thereafter that *no* significant probability attached to the proposition that the war would deal with or even begin to deal with Islamic terrorism in general. There was the opposite probability, that it would increase it, as so very many saw and said.

They could have added that it is often or always a dangerous policy, when you can't find the actual persons who attacked you, to attack some distantly related people. You are, after all, killing the wrong ones. They won't like it. Neither will those who feel with and for them. Many will fight back for this reason alone.

What of the idea that after 9/11 our American and British natures and societies were such that it was humanly impossible not to assert our civilization against a barbarian? Was it the case that America, having suffered the atrocity of 9/11, having suffered what is under-described as the affront and insult of that atrocity, had little choice? Was the case like Afghanistan, just after 9/11? Clearly it was not. Time had passed, getting on for a year and a half. You can stop merely reacting and start thinking of the best thing to do in that time. The war was not forced on America, nor of course Britain.

As for democracy as something to be bestowed on the Iraqis and a kind of guarantee of our own wisdom and rectitude in bestowing it, you will know I think there was the need to remember what our democracy actually is and what its general and greatest recommendation comes to. It is hierarchic democracy. In general it is better than dictatorship. There must be a hope that in some future decade Iraq will be better than it was under Saddam Hussein. But it is the democracy that denies to a large minority of its citizens many of the great human goods. It is a democracy that denies to the bottom tenth of its citizens so much that many of the rest of us can think of their lives as barely worth living.

Still, here with democracy for the Iraqis, as was not the case with the supposed need for self-defence from immediate attack, or the prevention of Islamic terrorism in general, we do have *a* reason for war, not a weightless consideration. That is not all that is to be said on the subject of democracy.

American and British hierarchic democracy took the United Kingdom into war without the democratically elected representatives in the second democracy, British Members of Parliament, being allowed to debate and vote on the question – as you have heard. This going to war as a whole, the process and event, the reality of the reason we are considering, is a summing-up or at least an excellent snapshot of our democracy. It might have been more considered in our earlier thinking on it.

It is as true that British democracy conceived as something other than our hierarchic and primitive system did *not* take the country into war. The democratic decision of the British, otherwise conceived, was *not* for war. As you will anticipate, I have in mind a democratic decision where that is something truer to the judgements and feelings of a people as a whole than in the case of the decision taken by hierarchic democracy. Such a democratic decision in a matter of overwhelming consequence, a matter of war and many deaths, will also be a clear one. Such a democratic decision in favour of war will not be uncertain, and perhaps not close. There was no such decision in Britain to make war on Iraq. About a million people marched against it. Rather, there was a reason of democracy *against* war.

At this point in our assembling of reasons for war we contemplated the idea that we already had enough to enable us to see that the end would justify the means. In fact, as I trust you will agree, those reasons could not be regarded as amounting to anything like a price worth paying. How many would die in the war? There was an awful uncertainty about that. Something else of a more general kind is as important.

You will remember that the Principle of Humanity is not well expressed as the idea that an end justifies certain means. Rather it is that an end and certain means may justify the means. Our leaders were not of such a moral attitude. In fact they were of another attitude. They were not thinking a lot, not enough, of the costs in the means. They did not know what those costs would be. They could not and perhaps would not judge that crucial fact. In fact our leaders *were*, as those of us given to the Principle of Humanity are *not*, doing something very like taking the end to justify the means in a terrible and culpable way. They were taken up with the end and not thinking enough of the costs of the means.

To come now to the reason for war that it was legal, remember our earlier thinking about international laws in general and international resolutions in particular. What we said is that what is legal is patently not necessarily what is right, but that some of the laws and resolutions, such as the body of UN resolutions against neo-Zionism, are of very considerable weight in judging right and wrong.

And thus the law and resolutions with respect to the war on Iraq? Whatever importance you would give to an international sanction for war, if it had existed, there was no such thing. There was, rather, American disdain for law and resolutions, and a British pretence of legality carried forward by a supine and unprincipled lawyer of the government. That is the judgement of all the world save for the personnel in question.

The continuation and aftermath of the war, further, would have in it at least something of the level of honourableness of the opening arguments for it. The continuation and aftermath could be low and might be bestial. The continuation and aftermath might be, as in fact they have been, violations of the Geneva and Hague Conventions and Protocols, the Nuremberg Charter of 1945, and the Rome Statute of the International Criminal Court. These violations have included conducting an aggressive war, indiscriminate killing, collective penalties as in the case of the killing of 600 women and children in Fallujah in 2004, failure to record deaths and injuries, use of chemical munitions, economic exploitation of occupied territories, torture, rape, sexual humiliation, religious humiliation, the use of dogs in particular, and merely partisan declarations by the American government purporting to suspend the Geneva Conventions.

The war waged by us against the Iraqis has therefore been terrorist war. There can be no alternative to this conclusion. The fact of its illegality contributes something to movement in the direction of a moral verdict on the war and our operations in its aftermath. Whatever anticipation of judgement you bring to the subject of terrorism on account of its illegality, you have as much or as little reason to engage in such anticipation with this terrorist war. The larger importance of this terrorist war, however, is that it must obstruct any verdict on terrorism, including any terrorism by Iraqis in Iraq, that is owed to an idea or supposition about any special or unique illegality.

To go on with our assembled reasons, say what you want of the alliance of the British government with the American one, Britain standing together with America. Assign some importance, in thinking of thousands of deaths in Iraq, to whatever benefit you suppose was conferred on the British people by its government playing what probably was a necessary part in bringing about the war. Would Bush and those around him have succeeded in taking America to war by itself? Whether or not, add in to our considerations the profit secured by the British government for the British people.

There was also the somewhat wider proposition, mentioned in passing, that all things considered the war could be judged to be in Britain's interest, that it was in accord with the politics of reality. One thing to be said of this now is that that judgement was one formed or shaped by the ideology of the New Labour Party. It was a matter of our interest from that point of view. Would any other judgement agree? None did. Nor, if the best informed and capable judgement had produced that verdict of *self-interest*, of course, would it follow that it was right.

To come now to the subject of ideology, you know something of my view of the political tradition of conservatism, enough to know a judgement to be made about what recommendation was conferred on the war by it. You will know, too, what can be said of oil, the dollar, and capitalism. We here have no clear recommendation of the war. We have nothing that has the ring of an argument for anything from the premise of the great human goods, the premise about bad lives that is the Principle of Humanity.

You know still better my view of the recommendation that was conferred on war by its being of very great service to neo-Zionism, to the further violation of Palestine and the Palestinians. And add what reflections you will on the political careerism of leaders and the contribution of so many members of the class of democratic politicians. You might have a look at Plato's *Republic* in that connection some time.

A summary is needed. The possible elements in a full explanation of our war on Iraq were a falsehood about imminent danger to us, a

proposition absurd and dangerous about the defeat of Islamic terrorism generally, a weak idea of necessity, a declaration about saving
a people from a dictator and therefore suffering, appeals about
hierarchic democracy, dishonourable effrontery about legality, an
alliance of uncertain relative value, the politics of reality, conservative ideology, thinking about oil and the corporations and so on,
neo-Zionism, and a political class.

Let us now move towards a conclusion.

There was a report in the *Guardian* a while ago of findings by two
independent research groups about deaths in Iraq. In the two years
since the invasion of Iraq, according to the report, 24,865 Iraqi civilians had been killed. 9,270 were killed by American, British and
other troops. About 8,950 were victims of the criminal violence, as
distinct from resistance by insurgents, owed to the social collapse
due to the war. 1,281 were children. At least 50 were babies. Other
counts and calculations of casualties have been much higher. It tran-
spires that there is considerable reason to accept medical research
published in *The Lancet* to the effect that there is a 90 per cent
chance that there have been more than 44,000 civilian deaths and a
50 per cent chance that there have been more than 98,000. Let us
say, again, 60,000. Or, if you want, just say 24,865.

Bush and Blair justify these killings. They do so, in large part, by
way of the reasons for war at which we have looked. They do so, in
another part, by a consideration that needs attention. It has been of
such importance that it will occupy us for a while.

It is the familiar line of thinking to the effect that these deaths
were not intended by Bush and Blair or by our men dropping the
bombs or firing the missiles. They did not intend to kill innocent
people. Their actions were not directed at the civilians. They would
have chosen, of course, to proceed in such a way as to avoid all
civilian deaths if that had been possible consistently with their own
safety. What our leaders and the men intended was the killing of
Iraqi soldiers and then insurgents. The deaths of innocents were not
of actual targets but rather, as you know, what American military
people call collateral damage.

This, you will allow me to say, is moral nonsense. It is worse than that. It is viciousness. It is the moral nonsense and viciousness about the deaths of innocents that is so useful here and elsewhere to our leaders. It is useful here in trying to defend a war and useful elsewhere in attacking terrorism.

What makes something right or wrong is what it will do. What makes something right or wrong, to speak a little more carefully, is what it is reasonably expected to do. It is nonsense to suppose that something is to be judged right as a result of ignoring some of what you know or believe it will do. This is on a level with supposing that a murderer who kills a husband in the course of achieving his aim or goal of killing the husband's wife is to be judged only in terms of the killing of the wife.

But let us think some more about the killing of innocents. Consider a young Palestinian woman who carries a bomb onto a bus in Israel to kill innocents and herself. Consider the American who fires a missile at a house or into the neighbourhood of a house said to have insurgents in it. In the house or thereabouts there are innocents, maybe a wedding party, and they are killed. What is typically said, as you know, is that there is a difference or a gulf between the two cases, because the American did not intend to kill innocent people.

It is true that there are ways of looking at the two actions that can be expressed in terms of intentions somehow conceived and that one or two of these ways do or may make a difference between them. The question is whether they make a difference of right and wrong. Is it that they are irrelevant to the question?

To say someone intended something in an action, or that somebody above them or commanding them intended something in the action, may be to say, roughly, that they foresaw the probable consequences of the action and went ahead. This is the way of looking at the thing, as you have heard before now, that does indeed make for the right or wrong of the action. It *is* what is relevant. This is not something peculiar to the Principle of Humanity, but common to most or many moralities and to most or much law.

As the casualty figures for innocents killed by American soldiers mount, and more innocent deaths are foreseeable and foreseen, it is impossible to make a difference between the action of an American soldier and the action of the Palestinian woman in terms of killing innocents – whatever else can be said of either of them. Both the American and those above him, as much as the Palestinian woman, intend in this way to kill innocents. Beyond question of doubt we here have a way of looking at the killing of innocents in terms of intention that makes no general difference or right and wrong between the two kinds of actions. It does nothing whatever to make the American action less wrong.

But, you say, it is true that in some other sense the Palestinian woman intended exactly what she did and the American didn't. Maybe you mean she actually saw her victims, saw them living and breathing, and went ahead anyway, and this was not true of him. But does that fact about the experience of two persons make a difference of right and wrong in their actions? How could it? It could not possibly do so, for many reasons. Killing *more* innocents horrifically but out of sight would by this supposition be less wrong than killing *fewer* innocents in sight. Anybody with a long-range sniper rifle or capable of planting a roadside bomb could thereby make his killing less wrong.

Do you say that on the way to the bus the woman had the forward-looking intention of killing innocents but the American on the way to the target did not? I wonder what you mean. Is it that she pictures her coming victims – that, as philosophers say, this was the representative content of her intention? And this was not so with the American? He pictured doing his duty, following orders, serving freedom, killing insurgents against it. But it is absurd to try to make any such general difference between the two. The Palestinian woman may picture serving the cause of her people or whatever. The American cannot put out of his mind by hypnosis that there are people in the buildings he is about to incinerate, and that they may not all be insurgents.

That similarity or sameness is not the main point, however. The main point is a little like an earlier one about acts and omissions.

Who really says, when they slow down to think about the thing, that you can kill twenty men, women and children horribly, which thing was a known possibility or probability, partly because you have fixed your mind on something else? No one to whom we need pay attention says this. They may have some other reason for justifying an action, but it cannot be this.

Maybe you are resolute and now repeat something already noticed, that the American and those above him, if they had the choice or possibility, would have chosen to kill the insurgents without killing any innocents. Well, it is certainly not always true that military people and those in charge of them choose to avoid civilian deaths. Sometimes they aim at them. It is claimed with reason that this has happened in Palestine. But suppose our sample American is just as supposed. He would prefer not to kill the innocents if he could, and so there is this sense in which he does not intend to kill them.

There is a clear reply. The Palestinian woman, if she had the choice or possibility, would have chosen without killing innocents to kill Sharon or Israeli soldiers or leading or committed neo-Zionists or to affect these people as much. Is any significant difference made by the fact that Sharon and so on are not going to be victims of her bomb along with the innocents? I leave you to work that out, maybe to come to thoughts about moral agents or moral personalities or whatever. What I have to say is that if it is known that two actions will or are likely to kill innocents, no difference of rightness is made between them by what either actor would have done instead if reality were otherwise than it was.

Is there hope, finally, in the simple idea that it was certain that the Palestinian woman would kill innocents but that there was only a chance or a probability that the American would kill some? That in this sense the American did not intend the deaths? Well, as a war goes on, and the numbers of dead innocents mounts, maybe day by day, this recourse becomes more or less impossible. The Americans may be known to be killing *more* innocents than their adversaries, whatever the probability that attaches to any particular attack. It is not merely possible but a fact that a president who orders a high probability of many thousands of innocent deaths is patently more in the wrong than anyone who with certainty acts so as to produce a few innocent deaths.

The short story, then, is that there is a way of looking at actions in terms of intention that is common, clear and inescapable. This way of looking at actions, in terms of foreseeable consequences, does indeed make for judgements of right and wrong. It does not make our actions in Iraq less wrong. It goes no way at all towards justifying them. It does not make a significant difference between the action of the Palestinian woman and the American. As against this, there are ways of looking at the actions that may or may not make a little difference between them, but are irrelevant to right and wrong.

Take another moment, before we go on, to remember something about definitions of terrorism. What was said earlier of defining terrorism as the intentional killing of innocents was that this by implication would assume that all terrorism is wrong, and would have certain counter-intuitive upshots, and would merely impede rather than make any significant difference to serious inquiry. More important, the definition would have a particular effect. In thinking of or discussing a war and terrorism, the definition would cheat by forcing the deaths of random innocents in terrorism on our attention and diverting us from the deaths of random innocents in war. It would do this with any war, including terrorist or criminal war. What needs remarking now is that the outstanding case in our history of this lowness is provided by the talk of governments of terrorism and the Iraq war.

We had Bush and Blair on our minds, and their justification of killings in Iraq. Let us return to them.

What they must do to justify the killings of the innocents in Iraq is to abandon weak stuff about intentions. What they must do is maintain that the killings have been worth it in terms of all the expected consequences – worth it on the basis of the best judgement as to all its probable effects. In terms of the Principle of Humanity, what is required in order to justify the killings is to show that in the best judgement it was rational to kill the 24,865 persons or the 60,000 or the 98,000 with respect to the end of keeping and getting people out of bad lives. The idea, I repeat, is morally vicious.

You will say I have strayed off the main point, and indeed I have. The main point is what could be judged of going to war in 2003, not what can be judged now. Well, the answer to that is that it could be judged in 2003 that a good many thousand Iraqi civilians would be killed, maybe 10,000, maybe more. So would a lot of soldiers, our young men with vulnerable bodies and families, like those who would take up arms against them. Whatever else was said about what would be a brief and easy war, this was what could be judged to be in some significant or great degree probable. Very many said so. It is relevant to the correctness of that judgement of probability, to put it no higher, that it is what turned out to be true.

Something needs to be made more explicit about that. There is a difference between (a) going to war and (b) not going to war with the danger that a dictator, maybe a cowed or now prudential dictator, will cause more suffering to people. The first course of action carries with it the dead certainty of killing and maiming many. The second carries only some probability that people will suffer. That is an elementary and crucial difference.

Given these propositions, no decent morality, no morality worth disputing with, could conclude that the reasons assembled for the war, that mess, could justify embarking on it. The morality of humanity condemns it. No decent morality, no morality above contempt, could justify our leaders and political parties who embarked on war. They have been deficient in moral intelligence. The morality of humanity condemns them absolutely. It places them on a level with bin Laden. It brings them together with Sharon. It joins them to Saddam Hussein. Bush and Blair are greater contributors than these to the killings.

They are also in that company for other reasons. They are there for their earlier contributions in the history that led to the war. They are there, in particular, for the fact of neo-Zionism, without which the war on Iraq would not have happened. Neo-Zionism stands in connection with it. They are there for not having got around to learning from the fact of 9/11. That failure in moral intelligence was also a necessary condition of the war on Iraq.

And the question of right and wrong now, of what to do now? It is not hard. It follows from what you have heard.

It follows from the photographs of naked men on leashes in the American prison in Baghdad, and the film of the savage beatings of young captives by British soldiers. This is barbarism, barbarism exactly, barbarism that trickles down from the leaders of two democracies. You make a mistake if you think a rich people cannot be a people of a barbarian government.

Of course we should take our armies and security guards and corporations and contractors out of Iraq. We should let the Iraqis have the government or governments they want, not the government we want for them, or the government that Texans and our oil strategists want for them. We in Britain should get decent leaders in the place of the ones we have, leaders who disdain the nonsense that the reasons our troops have been kept in Iraq are humanitarian ones, say the danger of civil war. The most likely thing about that proposition is that it is owed to self-interest, maybe reassuring and profitable self-deception.

We in Britain should not be quiet about our leader who by clanking repartee has joined us into the killing of the 24,865 or the 60,000 or the 98,000 people. We should not go back to political business as usual with him.

7/7 and the
Importance of Horror

11 March 2004 was a year after the beginning of the Iraq war, to which the Spanish government had sent 900 men. It was also three days before the Spanish national election. In Madrid on that day bombs were placed by Islamic terrorists on four commuter trains in Madrid. 191 people were killed. Many were maimed or had their lives made appalling or bad in other ways.

7 July 2005 was a day on which the leaders of the G8 group of rich countries, including Bush and Blair, were meeting in Edinburgh. There was some hope, after campaign concerts in various places by rock bands, that the G8 leaders would take a large step to relieve poor countries of their debts. In London on the day, suicide terrorists took bombs onto three subway trains, one onto the Piccadilly Line near Russell Square, one onto the Circle Line near Liverpool Street station, one onto the Circle Line near Edgware Road station. A bomb was also taken onto a No. 30 bus in Tavistock Square. In all, 56 people were killed and many more lives were made awful.

There is no reason for us to think of the English hellishness rather than the preceding Spanish one, or indeed of other terrorist attacks or attacks since 7/7. What prompts me to do so is the focus of our reflections mainly on the history and future of the English-speaking world, America and Britain in particular, the history and future of many readers of this book. Maybe it is no bad thing, either, for me to think about the terrorism of Russell Square and Tavistock Square. Those are places of my own life, where friends and acquaintances could have died, as did a woman who worked in the college of much of my past.

Here, from the *Guardian* newspaper, is an account of Sergeant Steve Betts of the British Transport Police, one of the first to reach the Piccadilly Line train.

It was pitch black and we had torches. The tunnel where the train was was about 150 metres down the track round a corner, and there were still a few wounded coming towards us as we approached. As I walked down the track, I heard someone cry out for help but I could not see them. I called out back and looked around but it was very smoky and dusty and they did not answer.

I got into the train and it was quite obvious that this was something horrendous. There were people with limbs missing, huge open wounds with their organs showing, and people were crying out and moaning and asking for help.

I thought, this is the worst thing I have ever seen. I am not very good in enclosed spaces at the best of times and we had to climb over bodies and body parts to try to help people and see who was still alive. I thought this is the end of the world, right here in this carriage, but you have to do your job.

I found a man and his left leg had been blown off below the knee, there was another body next to him. There was also what I thought was a pile of clothes but as I passed to try and get to the man, it moaned and asked me for help. It was a woman. She had all her limbs blown off. I think she died on the concourse.

We had not yet got into the carriage where the bomb had exploded but we had to get in there to make sure no one else was alive. That was a scene I cannot describe.

The roof had collapsed and we had to to almost crawl in. There were body parts everywhere, there was not one bit as far as I could see that was not covered with organs or blood or bits of body. I was squashed in by chairs and dead bodies as we searched for anyone alive. I could not help standing on things but I had to carry on and do my job. It was like [somebody had been] collecting a lot of shop dummies and then cutting them up, pouring black paint over them, and filling the carriage.

After a couple of hours, I came up. The station was pretty quiet by now but someone asked me for directions which made me smile and that made me feel more human. But, as I stood there I felt lonelier than I thought was possible, I just wanted to see a friend or somebody new and give them a hug.

What is the importance of horror, our response of horror revived by this account? It would be monstrous to say that it is feeling that has to be entirely subordinated to further thinking. Sergeant Betts had to do his job. But it is nobody's job later on to think and not to feel. It was not our job to come to think and not to feel about the Holocaust either, or the killings of children in Palestine, or the terrible proposition about a moral right, or 9/11, or the killings of tens of thousands of Iraqis after the invading and disordering of their country.

But if a response of horror, that feeling about a horror outside us in the world, although it is not to be replaced by thinking, it is not itself a response that has no thinking in it. In fact the response of feeling could not be such a thing. There is hardly any feeling without content, hardly any feeling that it is not about the nature of a thing, probably including how it came about and what it will do. *Why?* comes with what you may see, or hear of others seeing. Usually an answer comes too, about wrong or right. No doubt it comes to the executioner in a state of the United States as he watches his victim die. No doubt it comes to American and British Air Force pilots as a relief in the course of watching the film record of what they did on the ground in the course of their duties.

There are questions here about moral consciousness that we will not pursue, but not questions that have answers essential to our inquiry. Let us take forward with us a conviction of the importance of our horror, the fact that it enters into our seeing particular wrongs, and that the seeing cannot be unthinking. It brings in reasons, good or bad. We see or come to see inhumanities in some horrors, and they cannot but lead us to the subject of other things, maybe other wrongs. We do not have a choice about that if we think at all. We do not have a choice unless we have become so overcome by self-deception as to entirely avoid evidence with respect to what we want to believe, maybe as a result of what others want us to believe.

So with 7/7 you will after a while have to have other thoughts about other horrors in the world. You will have to do so with respect to such things as the remains of those Iraqis who lived in a poor neighbourhood of Baghdad until one day a few weeks after the war started. The journalist and author Robert Fisk went there.

> It was an outrage, an obscenity. The severed hand on the metal door, the swamp of blood and mud across the road, the human brains inside a garage, the incinerated, skeletal remains of an Iraqi mother and her three small children in their still-smouldering car. Two missiles from an American jet killed them all – by my estimate more than twenty Iraqi civilians, torn to pieces before they could be 'liberated' by the nation which destroyed their lives. Who dares, I ask, to call this 'collateral damage'? Abu Taleb Street was packed with pedestrians and motorists when the American pilot approached through the dense sandstorm that covered northern Baghdad in a cloak of red and yellow dust and rain yesterday morning.

You will, if you start with Russell Square and Tavistock Square, as all the world knows, even when it is pretending to think otherwise, have to consider Abu Taleb Street. If you want to go on making a great difference between them, you will have to tell yourself what it is. You will have to let yourself know why some horrors in the world to which you rarely can attend are not also given to you as wrongs, fail to be things that seem to have wrong written on them.

Almost all of us make differences between massacres. Certainly our leaders do it for us. What American soldiers do in Iraq, or British soldiers, when, as they say, things work out badly in an operation – those are horrors but for us they do not demand condemnation in the first moment of awareness of them, demand to be seen as evils. Yes, almost all of us are selective with horrors. We choose between horrors. We think of some differently than we do of others. You know my way of being selective, or of refusing to be selective. That is the morality of humanity, its first definition being by way of the Principle of Humanity.

So it could not be that the horror of 7/7 was other than that of a great wrong. It was as clearly the subject of the overwhelming thought that something had been done whose immediate consequences did indeed make it an atrocity, whose possible or conceivable consequences of justification could not be more than unconsidered hopes, close to fantasies that could not begin to excuse it. The Principle of Humanity condemns these bombings, and without qualification holds responsible those who carried them out.

That condemnation is not qualified by something else.

The leader of the 7/7 terrorists, Mohammad Sidique Khan, a teacher's assistant, made a videotaped statement to leave behind him. He said our support of our democratically elected governments, perpetrators of atrocities against his people all over the world, made us directly responsible for those atrocities, as he was directly responsible for the killings in the London Underground on behalf of his Muslim brothers and sisters. We cannot take our views from him. But we cannot be true to humanity if we let ourselves be silenced because certain propositions that force themselves on us are akin to his.

The wrong of Palestine is in the relevant past of what he and the others did. The wrong of Iraq, our terrorist war in Iraq, is a larger part in that past. Bush and Blair therefore share responsibility for 56 lives taken in London. So too does Osama bin Laden share that responsibility. So too did we contribute who follow our leaders.

The mistaken mention of 'direct responsibility' in the statement with respect to our own acts and omissions may with reason prompt you to say that Bush and Blair were not directly responsible for the deaths on 7/7. That is certainly true. Only Mohammad Sidique Khan and three others were directly responsible in the only defensible sense of the words. That is the fact, simply, whatever follows from it, that no other person's decision was part of the subsequent chain of events connecting their detonating of their bombs with the deaths.

A noted British moral philosopher, Bernard Williams, made the same distinction, speaking of someone's being only 'negatively responsible' for something terrible in the case where someone else's free decision was a subsequent part of the story. His example was of someone's refusing to shoot one man personally when under the threat that if he refused someone else would shoot not only the man in question but also a lot more.

Williams left it unclear why the earlier person should be less responsible for a terrible thing. But the matter is clear enough, and requires no obscurities about something other than the consequences of decisions, maybe about the role of autonomy, freedom or integrity in affecting responsibility for things. You may indeed refuse to kill someone in such situation for a plain reason. It is that there is a possibility, in fact a certain probability, that if you refuse, the threat of worse consequences will not be carried out. But what if the probability is high or very high that the second person will act? What if in ordinary terms it is *certain* that they will? That transforms the situation, and judgements of responsibility.

To return to Bush and Blair and others, it was asserted and reasserted by personnel of various kinds, some in our national intelligence agencies, before the attack on Iraq, that the attack would give rise to terrorism against us. It would not be a case of *if*, but of *when*. Here was a case, then, where a contribution to terrorist killings would be indirect or only negative, but where because of a probability, two leaders thereafter *did* share a responsibility for those killings.

No doubt this fact, seen by almost all, is the explanation of a second falsehood by Blair. That was to the effect that 7/7 had nothing to do with the terrorist war on Iraq. This ludicrous proposition was supported by dismal pieces of reasoning, notably that the terrorist attack of 9/11 had preceded Iraq, as had other terrorist attacks.

One thing that needs to be said of various inexplicit and weak ideas involved in this reasoning is that two causal circumstances for two terrorist attacks, say 9/11 and 7/7, like two causal circumstances for anything else, will typically be such that they are indeed similar, but one, say the later circumstance, will have a necessary part that is not contained in the earlier one. It may have in it, for example, a response of war to the earlier attack. It may have in it the Iraq war.

Another thing to be said is that while it is something like imaginable without self-contradiction, logically possible, that a second thing would or could have happened without a first, that is absolutely nothing to the point in reasoning about the world. For a start, empirical science exists, including psychology. So does ordinary reasoning unmotivated by a desire for exculpation or whatever.

The asserting or implying by Blair of the falsehood that 7/7 had nothing to do with the war on Iraq is of no effect whatever with respect to putting in doubt the probability of the connection between Iraq and 7/7. It is an extent of probability on which we act and need to act throughout our lives in endless circumstances, including punishment by the state, indeed punishment for real incitement. The asserting or implying of the falsehood *is* important in another way. It at least opens a question about our hierarchic democracies. Can a leader of one, you may ask, get away with self-serving nonsense? Is hierarchic democracy the kind of thing that is so habituated to compliance and deference that it can give a hearing to the inane?

The shares of responsibility of our leaders and those around them have to do with more than Palestine and Iraq. You will remember what was said of wider considerations in connection with 9/11, a context of wrong for our wrong of supporting neo-Zionism. Does the subject of a wider context with starvation in it irritate you? Does it strike you as a kind of intrusion into reflections that would be better or less bad without that intrusion?

You are, as you will know, in the company of someone whose commitments, translated into politics, are now what are called radical ones. As you have heard, it is possible to think that kinds and degrees of connection with the Principle of Humanity are what define the Left in politics. Is it easy for you, as a result, to put aside these latter ascriptions of responsibility having to do with a context?

It is worth remarking that with both the wrongs of Palestine and Iraq and also the larger context you will need to put aside more persons than radical or uncertain moral philosophers. You will have to put aside a multitude, probably a majority, with notable leaders. What your guide has contributed is more an attempt at articulation than invention, discovery or originality.

The Foreign Secretary of the United Kingdom for a time, Robin Cook, was a working politician and a realist. I suspect he spoke for most of the world, and for people of every known line of politics, when he made a certain judgement a year after the invasion and occupation of Iraq:

We would have made more progress against terrorism if we had brought peace to Palestine rather than war to Iraq.

To which he might have added later that we would have saved lives at Russell Square and Tavistock Square if we had dealt with Palestine rather than Iraq.

As for your scepticism having to do with the wider issues, the context of the wrongs of neo-Zionism and Iraq, you can contemplate the view of Peregrine Worsthorne. He is a true and clear voice of traditional conservatism in our time. He has no responsibility for any proposition whatever of mine, and is not associated with any by what is also true. It is that he could see and say a thing in a newspaper a week after 7/7. If my idea and maybe yours about the inevitability of the capitalism we have is not his idea, you may anyway find his words of interest.

Surely it is possible for a Muslim fundamentalist quite reasonably to see President Bush's aim of making the whole world safe for democratic capitalism as a no less mortal threat to his traditional way of life, or his traditional sacred values, as we saw the threats from Stalin and Hitler, or even from the Kaiser and Napoleon, as a mortal threat to our ways of life or sacred values. Once that effort of imagination is made, Muslim terrorism becomes understandable not so much as a rational act to turn back the irresistible forces of modern capitalism, but rather as a form of madness which has many historical precedents – particularly in the cause of national self-determination – many of which posterity applauds.

7/7 and Who are the
Enemies of this Terrorism?

Is it your idea, too, that you are in the company not only of a philosopher but also an apologist for terrorism? The terrorism that was 7/7 and 9/11? A sympathizer with this terrorism? A condoner of it? Too much of an understander of this terrorism? Too much of an endorser?

You have heard something already of the attitudes and the actions of the very many of us among whom I am. We take good care not to incite acts of terrorism by glorification or anything else, in order to go on getting a hearing for what we have to say. If we endorse the end and the means of Palestinian terrorism in Palestine, and endorse the end but not the means of such terrorism elsewhere, we incite this terrorism nowhere. We do not abandon reasoned argument or freely and strongly putting a case and engage instead in exciting, stirring, impassioning or enraging people into action in circumstances where such action is possible. We are resolute in holding to the value of argument, the value of reason as against the essentially emotive.

No doubt there is some self-preservation in this, particularly in a time of low government. You can have some self-concern about what you say when a government is in a way engaged not only in defending a society against terrorism but is also trying to reduce condemnation of itself, motivated by a particular ideology and infected by political calculation. With respect to the calculation, as you have heard before, a government can be resolute in trying to legislate against what it says is danger to the people in order by a kind of confusion about its resolution to imply that it was right to take that people into a war in which most of the people did not believe and do not believe.

But if there is self-preservation in not inciting, a disinclination to go to jail despite the inspiration of the philosophers Socrates and Bertrand Russell and of honourable people in other lines of life, there is also something else of greater force and importance. That is exactly what we have been considering, a reflective horror with respect to almost all terrorism. *That* can stop you from thinking of inciting.

But, you may ask, changing the subject, does our *endorsement* even of some goals of terrorism, in general those that are also the goal of the Principle of Humanity, not have a certain effect? Putting aside anything about means, does endorsement of some goals not contribute to the resolve of young men and women set upon a course of action? Could it not start one on that path, the path to Russell Square? And if so, why do we ratify those goals, knowing this effect? Are we not implicated in horror?

The first answer is that it *is* true that to justify or defend a goal of any possible terrorists, or to understand it in the way of Cherie Blair, may or will in one way increase the probability of horrors. In morality and truth, this has to be admitted. There is no way of separating any endorsing, understanding or otherwise assenting to or approving of the end from the possibility of contributing something to the likelihood of some people adopting wrongful means to the end. That this is not incitement does not affect the point.

The situation is exactly the same as it has been with virtually *any* judgement or principle whatever of morality, politics or religion in all of history. This has most certainly been true of the teachings of Christ. Much has been done in his name, as we are regularly reminded. So too have wrong means been taken by some as a result of affirmations of freedom, equality, justice, democracy, need, human rights, and UN resolutions. So too with the politics of reality, a homeland, the tradition of a people, law, ethnic hope, and whatever else. People have died as a result in part of endorsements accepted then or later by half the world, indeed as good as the entire world.

Were none of these judgements ever to be heard? As remarked earlier, to prohibit such judgements, to prohibit what can issue in mistake, would be to prohibit nothing less than what is essential to the intelligent conduct of our existence. It is close enough to true that anyone who says something is or was right is doing what may have entirely undesired and grim consequences.

Still, you may ask again, why speak for the goal or end of the terrorism in question? There is a short reply, known to many and probably to you. Endorsing, understanding or otherwise approving of the goal of those terrorists who are first of all concerned with Palestine is to do several things. Yes, it is in a way to run a risk, the risk we are considering. It is also to do something else. It is in a way rightly to decrease rather than increase the probability of such horrors as 7/7 and 9/11.

It should be no surprise to you that a single thing can be part of two real stories, part of two causal circumstances, where the two circumstances have different and opposed effects. The fact is as simple as that the same weather can make for a good weekend in my case and a bad one in your case, or a partly good and a partly bad weekend in one case. It is as simple as that there are different hearers of Christ, different followers of Muhammed, different readers of books.

And, to come towards the conclusion of this line of reply, the endorsing or other approving of the goal of some terrorism, which admittedly does or may in a way increase such terrorism, may also in the other way do *more* to decrease this terrorism. Let me say that again. To be honest about a justified goal of some terrorism and to condemn the means is in a way to make more such terrorism likely and in a way to make it less likely – and by dealing with causes to do more of the second than the first.

Moreover, and crucially, to approve a goal of such terrorism as that of 7/7 and 9/11 and to condemn the means may indeed be to do more, *much more*, to make it less likely than just to condemn the means. That is the crux.

The likelihood of the terrorism we are considering will almost certainly last as long as its causes. It will last as long as some of us deny them. The Hundred Years War between England and France was unlikely. It happened. There is the possibility, a probability, of A Hundred Years of Terrorism against us. It will exist so long as we are misled by our democratic politicians and their makers.

It is time, perhaps, for a connected question from me rather than from you. We have been thinking of what we have called endorsers, understanders, apologists, sympathizers, condoners and so on of the terrorism with which we have been concerned. Let us now have the idea of *an actual enemy of this terrorism*, such terrorism as that of 7/7 outside of Palestine.

Such an enemy takes rational steps that actually reduce the prospect of this terrorism, whatever steps he or she can. The ideal character he or she aspires to be is someone who depends on the best knowledge and judgement in order to take rational steps against this terrorism. Such steps will in my view also be steps in accordance with the Principle of Humanity. But leave that if you want. Have in mind only some or other morality of decency, one that gives some precedence to reducing lives of distress and the like.

Who in fact are these actual enemies of the terrorism of 7/7 and 9/11? Who is as effective an enemy as can be, someone who does all within their powers to stop terrorism? Whether these be powers of information, argument, influence, money, authority, elected office, democratic certification, or prime ministerial or presidential command? There is no problem about that.

These actual enemies of terrorism are those of us who see the need to be concerned both with the terrorism and its causes. More than that, we are not attached to its causes. We are not implicated in them. We do not have distorting investments of several kinds in them. We have not got committed to them. Our self-identities are not bound up with them. Nor are we resigned about misery and inhumanity. We are not blinded or confused by self-serving ideas of the possible and the necessary and the realistic and the speakable. We are for *all* the steps of which the foreseeable consequence is less of the horror.

I say for us too that we are not unrealistic. We are not simple people. We know the possibility of a government coming close to suborning the police to secure useful judgements from them about the danger of terrorism, or simply pretending that the natural desires of the police for fewer restraints on their operations are something more objective. We are not merely empathetic either. We are not merely emotional. We are pretty good at argument. There are multitudes of us, too many for us to be naïve. We stand in a larger tradition of sense and decency than most of our politicians, a tradition into which the New Labour Party strayed for a while in terms of its speeches when it said it was tough on crime and tough on the causes of crime.

Are you reading these words, Blair? You are not an actual enemy of the terrorism of Russell Square. You are attached to its causes. You are an actual friend to this terrorism. You are an actual friend to the killing of innocent people. I am not. You are. You should stay away from memorial services. You are taking steps of which the foreseeable consequence is likely to be more of this horror rather than less. Your stuff about not giving in, not emboldening terrorists by making concessions, is merely factitious, and very likely motivated by a commitment to and identification with our wrongs. You can always *say* concessions will worsen things, however right they are.

Has someone paraphrased one or two of these words for you, Bush? Have a look yourself. Try to think a little about them. They're not all that hard.

The Spanish voted José María Aznar out of office three days after the Madrid bombings. British democracy later returned Blair to office with a greatly reduced majority. It is actually time, whether or not I waste words in saying it, that we need to try to get rid of Blair and Bush before their chosen times of departure. That might accelerate the learning process of their successors. We could try to stop the next election by mass civil disobedience, in the aim of getting a democracy better than hierarchic. We could begin by trying to unsettle that most destructive of conventions, the one that ordains what is realistic, what is possible, what can be thought. It isn't a dream any more that mass civil disobedience has a chance of working. Remember Poland, Germany, Georgia and Ukraine. It could be a start towards less horror in the world. Fewer bad lives in general too.

Our Societies and the War on Terror

This inquiry is as good as ended, but a couple of recurrent subjects can do with some attention. One can do with recollecting, bringing together and summing up. That is the subject of our societies as they are. America, Britain, Germany, France, Japan and those other societies that are like and with us. Each, you can say, is people being together in a place in a more or less organized way, subject to state and government, with a distribution of great and other goods owed to a level of moral and other intelligence as well as an economic system, and with a culture that may have religion in it, a culture owed to and supporting the other sides of the society.

The subject might have come up more than it did with Palestine. Neo-Zionism is ready enough to call for support not only because it is a sort of democracy but also because it is for a society something like ours. It is, as Netanyahu can say, part of *civilization*. There is the implication that the Palestine it replaced was not such a thing and that a real state for the Palestinians might not be.

As for 9/11, bin Laden and those of his mind justified it partly by way of a damnation of our societies and our spreading them to the rest of the world. We on the other hand take ourselves to be engaged not only in defending our societies against their adversaries, engaged in self-preservation, but in defending good societies with decent or half-tolerable leaders. It was and remains a part of the supposed justification of the invasion and occupation of Iraq that we are bringing the gift of our way of life to the Iraqis. As for 7/7 and other such inhumanities, those who seek to justify them do indeed include the proposition that we propose to export our way of life, which they despise, and that we are engaged in exporting it by means of death and destruction.

You know already that if I do not propose to emigrate to a dictatorship or to a theocratic, clerical or religious society, I am not whole-hearted in celebration of the different way we live.

What I myself have had to say, to look back over the course of our inquiry, is first that we have societies with leaders who say they go by international law but make it up when it suits them. Evidently they have other purposes. Our societies are societies that have tolerated and more than tolerated the object of United Nations Security Council resolutions, neo-Zionist Israel. We do not respect the human rights of our own citizens, and make do with speeches in connection with the destruction of the human rights of other peoples. Our societies make do with speeches about that loss of living time by the Africans. They are societies for whose governments the theory of the just war is occasionally a tool.

Our societies arise from conservatism and liberalism, ideologies incapable of either clarifying or recommending themselves, now intent on or tolerant of the further profitization of all social relationships. Our societies, once rightly thought of in terms of a kind of partnership between democratic and economic freedoms, and then necessarily in terms of what was called the consortium, are now things such that none of education, medical treatment, local government or whatever else has clear aims of truth and what is right. That life is not commercial life is overlooked.

Ours are societies whose natures are owed to hierarchic or primitive democracy, that sort of equality and freedom. It is a kind of government that can be led by lying or worse than lying, and can re-elect war-mongers, if with a smaller majority. They are societies whose leaders may seek new laws against free expression partly for an odious reason now clearer than when it was mentioned earlier. They seek the laws partly in order to point to a danger that must have been around for a while, with the purpose of obscurely implying a justification of their own past conduct, their starting what would be a bestial war.

Now, with the spring of 2006 coming, my own society's inhumanity comes into focus again. The leader of the party of liberals can point out to the party in government, the New Labour Party, descended from the party that made the actual fact of civilization that was the National Health Service, that the English poor are now poorer than they were under Thatcher, and still getting poorer. So with America. In America too the president follows the well-tried policy of keeping in touch with occasional dips in the credulousness of his fellow citizens. He gives up a falsehood about Iraq not because it is false but because it is no longer useable. In America too, public intellectuals and risen journalists still parade the memory of Saddam Hussein in order to justify our killing of the 24,865, 60,000 or 98,000.

To come now to a general characterization, our societies are exactly offences against humanity, against that decency that gets a good formulation in the Principle of Humanity's concern with bad lives. Long lives are not had by our poor. Their life expectancies, if not African, are still of a certain kind – such that we the well-off, if we were threatened with the prospect of our children and grandchildren having the same average lifetimes, would kill to prevent it. In our societies, there are those who live in pain that a little money could deal with, those whose lives are denials of freedoms of most kinds. There are those who are not able to be connected to the rest of us but are separated from us by the resentment and worse that must arise from seeing through shams. There are those who are born to live with disdain. There are the ignorant who have a sense of the vacuity of the television they watch for want of better.

This is not the necessary way, or the way things have always been in all places. It is an arrangement for the benefit of the rest of us, some of us far more than others. In Britain, it is now the arrangement that is maintained by the pompous effrontery of a government that eschews and is against rational means to the end of humanity. It puts in their place, at this time, talk about *reform* and *modernization* in a society.

Linger for a moment with me on this matter of words, although by the time you read this book, a new verbiage will very likely have been devised or come in. Reality pokes its way through mere talk and requires its regular replacement. A reform is a change in something that improves it, a good change. Of course a change does not become good by being *called* a reform. A modernization, I guess, satisfies present rather than past needs. Of course something does not satisfy present needs by being *named* a modernization. Is there point in my visiting these truisms on you? There is. It is exactly through naming, through declaration, through sonorous utterance of a term, that we are to be taught by our government and to learn.

The two baptismal names purport to have to do with economics. I keep up a bit with economics and its theory, although from the outside. I have never heard myself of what we ought to have heard of very often if it exists, a worked-out argument that private enterprise in hospitals or education or the like is actually more efficient than public enterprise, that competition is better than co-operation. I haven't heard an actually relevant definition of efficiency.

The more efficient enterprise is generally spoken of in economics as one that produces a greater output per unit of input of some kind. But if greater efficiency is really to be the test of whether to choose one method over another, output will need to include *all* the consequences of the method, the total end result. What might this end result be with respect to private and public enterprise? It will need to be specified and defended. What end might it be? Unquestionably a relevant definition of efficiency cannot have to do with just some *total* of economic activity or progress, with nothing said of who and what number of people benefit or suffer from the activity or progress.

If in our societies we are taught and are to learn by just the utterance of the words *reform* and *modernization*, so we are taught and are to learn just by the utterance of the word *terrorism*. We are to be taught and learn that we are rightly to kill and be killed in what we are not to think of or hear spoken of as *terrorist war* or *criminal war*. We are to kill and be killed by the great argument that is the utterance of the word *democracy*.

You will know that I do not myself think that our societies can much cite themselves in explanation and defence of their official views on Palestine, 9/11, Iraq, and 7/7, and what has already followed them. Ours are not ways of living that commend our views.

Do you say that this is a diatribe about our societies that reveals and identifies your guide as not only a kind of radical but as an ideologue himself? Or a mere moralist? Someone who should not have been let out of his ivory tower? Well, diatribe or not, it does identify him, and maybe it invites those several labels. And what identifies you? Something does, and very likely your convictions will be feelingful if you are open about them. But such argy-bargy between us doesn't matter much. You were here for a kind of inquiry, here to look into things, here to hear what can be said for some propositions, here to follow some arguments.

That's still what you need to engage in and think about, isn't it? Has it turned out, by way of your moment of perception of your guide, that the UN resolutions against neo-Zionism can be ignored as irrelevant pieces of international politics? Can you now conclude that in a democracy or whatever freedom doesn't depend on equality after all, that the two things aren't connected? Has it become clear that it is really only the ends that justify the means? That you can simply define your way into a condemnation or celebration of terrorism that requires attention? That if I burn you to death in a skyscraper that is OK because while I knew that could happen I was keeping in mind instead that I was serving a clean religion? That Abu Taleb Street is less real than Russell Square?

These thoughts on our societies prompt a postscript, on our War on Terror. It too, if it has been in view before, can do with summing up.

This thing led by the United States is indeed in one part an attempt to prevent such terrorist attacks against us as 9/11 and 7/7. This we try to do by gathering intelligence, arresting suspects, flying some of them to torturers elsewhere in order to have our hands look less dirty, convicting and imprisoning the guilty and those who incite them, imprisoning and torturing others never brought before a court, and trying to intimidate others.

We have also conducted our War on Terror by means, exactly, of making odinary war ourselves – terrorist war. This was the terrorist war on Iraq. It may be that our War on Terror will come to include ordinary war against Iran. This is unlikely to have the sanction of

international law as with the war on Iraq. Thus it too will be terrorist war. More important, any war on Iran is as good as certain to be
a further violation of the Principle of Humanity. It will be maiming,
death and the rest. The same is to be said, of course, of what has also
been threatened, a terrorist attack on Iran's nuclear facilities by neo-
Zionist Israel. It is in fact a ludicrous convention of our societies that
this real and serious threat and intention, not mere speechifying, is
tolerated by us.

Do you dutifully contemplate in this connection that a terrorist
war or attack on Iran may have the recommendation that it will
make the world a safer place? That it may prevent Iran from coming
to have nuclear weapons such as are now possessed by its neigh-
bours, most relevantly neo-Zionist Israel? As against this, there is a
plain argument from consistency for Iran's having nuclear weapons,
beginning from exactly the possession of nuclear weapons by neo-
Zionist Israel.

Arguments from consistency can always be resisted by one consideration, invention, piece of nonsense or another. The real endeavour in advancing an argument from consistency is always the
analysis of such considerations and what-not. The argument from
consistency for Iranian nuclear weapons most certainly cannot be
resisted by easy assumptions of an uneven distribution of rationality
and restraint among peoples and nations. In general, such assumptions must be absurd. Nor can the argument even be touched by the
convention that we who have the bomb are responsible people and
do not make wrong and awful war, a convention so absurd at the
present time as to shade into social amnesia.

It is my inclination to think something that it is too late to look
into here, that factual propositions and the Principle of Humanity
issue in the conclusion that Iran has as much right to get nuclear
arms as the Palestinians have had a right to defend themselves
against neo-Zionism. I offer the propositions for your consideration.

To revert to our War on Terror generally, the thing is owed to
more than the intention of preventing terrorist attacks on ourselves
by means including terrorist war. It shares many reasons and causes

with the war on Iraq. They include our moral superiority as societies and a civilization, hierarchic democracy, the end justifying the means, legality, ideology, national self-interest, neo-Zionism, a political class. A larger fact about the War on Terror, the largest fact, is that it is indeed a war on terror that does *not* include a war on the causes of terror — the defensible causes of terror that may or may not be defensibly pursued. Our War on Terror is a war that makes its own savagery more necessary by failing to attend to what requires attention. Our War on Terror is thus not a war being conducted by true enemies of terror, those who take all rational steps against it. Our War on Terror is being conducted by friends of that terror against us, friends too of what is to come.

Uncertainty and the Effect of Not Judging

You have heard of the recommendation of philosophy that it is a general logic, and heard that we can have what we need, a general principle that does much to keep a morality honest and fair, and that this Principle of Humanity has a moral truth that is a consistency with factual truths about our human natures. We have also agreed, I take it, that there are things that are beyond question, such as the datum of the wrong of torturing a child for sexual excitement.

It is discomfiting that there is more to remember. To think over some moral and political philosophy, say that of Rawls in his decent intentions or of Nozick making use of talk of liberty, is indeed to see that it is advocacy, that there are kinds of desire or inclination in it, and also resolution and will. Plainly, too, and more generally, it needs keeping in mind that a morality is an attitude or set of attitudes, where an attitude, even if it is supportable, has in it more than propositions of ordinary fact. It has a want in it, whether or not appearing as a value.

These thoughts can issue in, or more likely be used in, explanation of a certain proposition. You will remember hearing that if we come to an adequate view of right and wrong and a confidence about the facts of a situation, we do not have a choice about what follows as a judgement of right or wrong. We can stick to the conclusion as well as the premises, or give up both the conclusion and the premises. There isn't a third way. Was that summary a little too quick?

Did that assertion of the necessity of moral conclusions pass by a way in which they are *not* necessary? That some kind or other of lack of necessity is well enough shown by what is a possible or a likely response to the proposition that the Palestinians have had and do have a moral right to their terrorism in their homeland against the violation of it and of them? The response is that someone can somehow accept the premises and deny the conclusion. Someone can accept the morality of humanity and also the factual premises and deny the conclusion. The situation will be the same, of course, with those other conclusions that are the justification of Zionism and the condemnations of neo-Zionism, 9/11, the Iraq war, and 7/7.

Well, this common response faces a difficulty touched on earlier, several times. If the conclusion of a Palestinian moral right comes from the premises, the general moral premise also owes something to the conclusion. If the premise is not so dependent on the proposition of a Palestinian moral right as it is on such propositions as the one about the torturing of a child, the premise does have a source in the proposition of a moral right. It is on the way to being clear and true, then, that the morality of humanity is to be *understood* as the morality that along with relevant facts does have the moral right as a consequence. So with the conclusions about 9/11 and so on.

That leaves open a possibility that needs to be granted. It is that a morality different from but akin to the morality of humanity could be set out and that it would not issue in the proposition of moral right – or the condemnation of 9/11. There could be another *morality of concern*, to gesture at a group of moralities by the use of that name, that would not justify, say, the self-defence of the Palestinians.

These moralities, certainly, are not any of the bodies of thinking or practices put aside in the beginning, from negotiation and international law to democracy. Nor are moralities of concern to be confused with the deontological moralities with which the consequentialism of the Principle of Humanity was contrasted. Nor do they include utilitarianism. Rather, they are moralities that somehow have to do with acting against deprivation, distress and suffering rather than anything else.

If that is clear enough, and a required concession, there are other things as clear. You have heard a lot of explanation of the morality of humanity and a lot of argument for it. That fullness and explicitness, of course, makes it more open to examination than anything else unarticulated and undefended, something gestured at. But there can be no actual contest between something set out for examination and something gestured at. Let us have the alternative, please. It would be faced by and have to deal with almost all the challenges that can be offered to the morality of humanity, and also a challenge to what makes it different from that morality.

It is my conviction, and maybe yours, that if the thing were produced, it would be clear that the morality we have is superior to it, maybe demonstrably so. The morality of humanity has firm foundations. It is a morality of consistency. It does not license selective horror. It is resolute in that respect. It does not choose to overlook or forget or make less of some horrors. It has no smell of self-interest about it, no indeterminacy, obscurity or pomp that raises suspicion of self-interest. It is not tainted by convention, let alone mired in it.

Is the concession that in a certain way our conclusions have not been necessary ones a reason for standing back from judgement? Is it a reason for the comfort of not accepting the moral right of the Palestinians to their terrorism – or perhaps, you need to remember, a reason for not accepting the condemnation of the terrorism of 7/7? Can you omit to judge, omit to come to a verdict, omit to say what is of clearest and greatest force in support of the Palestinians and in judgement of neo-Zionism?

You can, but you will not need reminding, I hope, that you cannot thereby choose not to have an effect. On the contrary, you do have an effect by standing back. Omissions have effects. No one denies that a doctor's failing to keep someone alive has the effect that the person dies, and indeed that my keeping my money has the effect that other people die. In not judging that the Palestinians have their moral right, you have a certain effect on their situation. In comparison to your judging, you do something to contribute more than you might to the vicious inhumanity that continues to deny them what we all justify for ourselves.

You can have another idea, too, about a division of labour different from the one with which we began. That was the division of labour on large questions of right and wrong where the different labourers are historians, inquirers into international relations, philosophers, good journalists and others. Another division of labour, whose recognition has to be shown as somehow consistent with your own moral confidence, and mine, is the one where the different labourers are proponents and defenders of different moral positions and indeed moralities, not to mention mere partisans. We can be obliged to keep at our work.

Postscript on Anti-Semitism

This inquiry now ended had a predecessor, the book called *After the Terror*, published by Edinburgh University Press. It had very little do with Palestine, only six pages in 160, much more to do with Africa and the rest of the world. However, it did have in it the assertion that the Palestinians have had a moral right to their terrorism. The book was translated into German by the prominent publisher SuhrkampVerlag. When it was published, an open letter to the publisher appeared in a Frankfurt newspaper. It was by one Mischa Brumlik, the director of an institute having to do with the Holocaust and a professor of pedagogy at Frankfurt University. The book, he said, principally because of what it said of the Palestinians' moral right, was anti-semitic.

The next day the newspaper carried a piece from the leading German philosopher, the liberal Jürgen Habermas. He said he had recommended the book to Suhrkamp for translation, and he had read it again last night, and it was not anti-semitic. This he said, however, in the way of many or anyway some Germans in the neighbourhood of a charge of anti-semitism, with an unease that was close to apology. It was not a performance envied by all of the philosophers of his country.

He said of me, by the way, if you will let me linger on his words for a moment, 'He does not distinguish his political evaluation of Palestinian terrorism from the moral justification of it.' This is puzzling. Does it imply that something can be politically but not morally justified? Maybe that the politics of reality is somehow implicit in my outlook? Maybe he should read the book again.

Very obviously I take into account the question of whether Palestinian terrorism will work, which includes such considerations as its effects on opinions, attitudes, support of third parties, etc. This, presumably, is a political evaluation. So too, presumably, is a judgement of the necessity of Palestinian terrorism, the question of whether there are alternatives, no doubt negotiation. It is odd somehow to recommend *distinguishing* these evaluations from the moral evaluation of Palestinian terrorism – they are part of it. Prof. Habermas cannot contemplate that political considerations – the necessity of courses of action and so on – do not enter into moral judgement on them? No doubt we should read his works.

The day after his piece appeared, Suhrkamp Verlag 'banned' the book, which banning transpired to amount to not reprinting it. The Frankfurt newspaper then carried a piece by me, an open letter to Frankfurt University. The conclusion was the demand that Brumlik be sacked for a disservice to truth and decency that was not consistent with academic principle.

There was then a widening firestorm of controversy in Germany, or anyway the German media. There were riot police needed at a lecture in Leipzig. The story came to an end, or one end, with the retranslation and republication of the book in Germany, by Melzer Verlag. Its proprietor, Abraham Melzer, is a German, an Israeli, and a Jew. Also a man of honour and courage.

There have been lesser episodes of the same sort. One, with a beginning involving a member of my own past philosophy department at University College London, was resolved by the payment of legal costs, an apology, etc. Another episode, involving royalties that were to go to the British part of the charity Oxfam, whose deputy director gave in to a neo-Zionist threat from a Canadian newspaper, was more or less resolved by the judgement on him of the British press.

Some Palestinians, for their part, have condemned my Zionism as ignorant and contemptible. They have taken steps to stop its being heard in a London college or two. They take me as no friend. Some others on the Left in Britain have also vilified this Zionism, and established that I was wrong on all counts, notably in making a distinction between Zionism and neo-Zionism. Would that offending both sides of a conflict ensured truth.

It is one of the intentions of the libel of anti-semitism that it be taken seriously. Having done that for a while, I now decline to do so. Anti-semitism is hostility or prejudice against Jews in general. Things need to be added to the dictionary definition to catch the difference in nature between anti-semitism and hostility and prejudice against other people and nationalities. Anti-semitism is not like hostility to or prejudice against Germans or Americans.

One thing in anti-semitism is vileness about personal and bodily qualities of Jews. Another is a belief about the selfish manipulation of the societies they are in by all Jews, all of whom also remain separate from the societies. Another thing may be the imputation that Jews generally have neo-Zionist inclinations. Still more important is something else. It is the connection of anti-semitism with an historical fact and approval or toleration of it, maybe silence about it. That fact is the Holocaust.

It is my own view that the libel of anti-semitism is principally a side of neo-Zionism or a want of perfect detachment from it. The libel is useful in trying to take more Palestinian land. You, reader, are in a position to know something of whether you have been in the company of an anti-semite, what Brumlik called a Jew-hater. Think back on what you have heard. I trust you, and truth.

11 March 2006

Acknowledgements

In this book's recent history are lectures and talks at the Edinburgh Festival, the Bath Festival, the Gothenberg Festival, Bath University, Hamburg University, Bremen University, Birkbeck College London, the London School of Economics, University College London, Southampton University, Cork University, Lund University and the Catholic University of Brussels. Good questions were asked. I am also grateful for written comments to readers of all or part of a penultimate draft of this book, who are not to be taken as sharing my views. None shares all. They are Shahrar Ali, Iain Atack, Robin Blackburn, Scott Burchill, Ron Chrisley, Charles Crittenden, Tam Dalyell, Ovadia Ezra, John Gardner, James Garvey, Paul Gilbert, Ian Gilmour, Alastair Hannay, Virginia Held, Beland Honderich, Ingrid Honderich, John Honderich, Lee Hooker, Miroslav Imbrisevic, John Jones, Tomis Kapitan, Brian Klug, Hanif Kureishi, David Lewis, Kevin Magill, William McBride, Georg Meggle, Caroline Michel, Michael Neumann, Richard Norman, Bhiku Parekh, Thomas Pogge, Igor Primoratz, Tom Rockmore, Timothy Shanahan, Saul Smilansky, Slav Todorov, and Leo Zaibert.

More Reading

These books and shorter writings, by me and by others, enlarge on the sections of this book and sometimes disagree. Roughly the order in which their subjects come up in the sections of the book is the order in which the items are listed here. They are also sources of my history and statistics.

Our Questions

Ted Honderich, *After the Terror*, 2nd edn, Edinburgh University Press, 2003, pp. 30–39.

A Division of Labour, Philosophy's Part

Hugo Adam Bedau, 'Political Philosophy, Problems of', in Ted Honderich (ed.), *The Oxford Companion to Philosophy*, Oxford University Press, 2005.

Noam Chomsky, *Pirates and Empires, Old and New: International Terrorism in the Real World*, Pluto Press, 2002.

Justin McCarthy, *The Population of Palestine: Population History and Statistics of the Late Ottoman Period and the Mandate*, Columbia University Press, 1990.

Anthony Quinton, 'Philosophy', in Ted Honderich (ed.), *The Oxford Companion to Philosophy*, Oxford University Press, 2005.

Michael Slote, 'Moral Philosophy, Problems of', in Ted Honderich (ed.), *The Oxford Companion to Philosophy*, Oxford University Press, 2005.

Rowan Williams, *Writing in the Dust: Reflections on September 11th and its Aftermath*, Hodder & Stoughton, 2002.

Negotiation, International Law

Ian Atack, *The Ethics of Peace and War*, Edinburgh University Press, 2005.

M. Cain and A. Hunt (eds), *Marx and Engels on Law*, Academic Press, 1979.

Antonio Cassese, *International Law*, 2nd edn, Oxford University Press, 2005.

Martin Dixon, *Textbook on International Law*, 5th edn, Oxford University Press, 2005.

Richard K. Gardiner, *International Law*, Pearson Longman, 2003.

Virginia Held, 'Terrorism, Rights, and Political Goals', in R. G. Frey and Christopher Morris (eds), *Violence, Terrorism and Justice*, Cambridge University Press, 1991.

Michael Neumann, *The Rule of Law: Politicizing Ethics*, Ashgate, 2002.

Bhikhu Parekh, *Gandhi: A Very Short Introduction*, Oxford University Press, 2001.

James P. Sterba, 'Terrorism and International Justice', in J. P. Sterba (ed.), *Terrorism and International Justice*, Oxford University Press, 2003.

UN Resolutions

'A List of United Nations Resolutions Against Israel', *Middle East News and World Report*, www.MiddleEastNews.com.

David Hirst, *The Gun and the Olive Branch*, 2nd edn, Faber & Faber, 1984.

Human Rights

Megan Addis and Penelope Morrow, *The Liberty Guide to Human Rights*, Pluto Press, 2000.

David Beetham (ed.), *Politics and Human Rights*, Blackwell, 1995.

Jack Donnelly, *International Human Rights*, Westview, 1998.

Thomas W. Pogge, 'Recognized and Violated by International Law: The Human Rights of the Global Poor', *Leiden International Law Journal*, 2005.

R. J. Vincent, *Human Rights and International Relations*, Cambridge University Press, 2005.

Just War Theory

Iain Atack, *The Ethics of Peace and War*, Edinburgh University Press, 2005.

Mark Evans (ed.), *Just War Theory: A Reappraisal*, Edinburgh University Press, 2005.

Timothy Shanahan (ed.), *Philosophy 9/11: Thinking About the War on Terror*, Open Court, 2005.

The Politics of Reality

Scott Burchill, *Theories of International Relations*, 3rd edn, Palgrave Macmillan, 2005.

James P. Sterba, 'Terrorism and International Justice', in James P. Sterba (ed.), *Terrorism and International Justice*, Oxford University Press, 2003.

Conservatism and Liberalism

Ian Gilmour, *Inside Right: A Study of Conservatism*, Quartet, 1978.

Ted Honderich, 'Conservatism, Its Distinctions and Its Rationale', in *On Political Means and Social Ends*, Edinburgh University Press, 2003.

Ted Honderich, 'John Stuart Mill's *On Liberty*, and a Question About Liberalism', in *On Political Means and Social Ends*, Edinburgh University Press, 2003.

Ted Honderich, *Conservatism: Burke, Nozick, Bush, Blair?*, Pluto Press, 2005.

Ted Honderich, 'A Theory of Justice, an Anarchism, and the Obligation to Obey the Law', in *Terrorism for Humanity: Inquiries in Political Philosophy*, Pluto Press, 2005.

John Stuart Mill, *On Liberty*, in J. Gray and G. W. Smith (eds), *On Liberty In Focus*, Routledge, 1991.

John Rawls, *A Theory of Justice*, Harvard University Press and Oxford University Press, 1971.

Democracy's Equality

Noam Chomsky, *Necessary Illusions: Thought Control in Democratic Societies*, Pluto Press, 1989.

Robert A. Dahl, *A Preface to Democratic Theory*, University of Chicago Press, 1956.

Robert A. Dahl, *Modern Political Analysis*, 5th edn, Prentice Hall, 1991.

Ted Honderich, 'Hierarchic Democracy and the Necessity of Mass Civil Disobedience', in *On Political Means and Social Ends*, Edinburgh University Press, 2003.

Ted Honderich, 'Trying to Save Marx's Theory of History by Teleology, and Failing', in *On Political Means and Social Ends*, Edinburgh University Press, 2003.

Ted Honderich, *Conservatism: Burke, Nozick, Bush, Blair?*, Pluto Press, 2005.

Greg Palast, *The Best Democracy Money Can Buy*, Pluto Press, 2002.

Democracy's Freedom

David Held (ed.), *Political Theory Today*, Polity, 1991.

Richard Norman, 'Does Equality Destroy Liberty?', in Keith Graham (ed.), *Contemporary Political Philosophy*, Cambridge University Press, 1982.

Ian Shapiro and Casiano Hacker-Cordon, *Democracy's Value*, Cambridge University Press, 1999.

Democracy's Help

Ted Honderich, 'The Contract Argument in a Theory of Justice', in *On Political Means and Social Ends*, Edinburgh University Press, 2003.

The Principle of Humanity

Ted Honderich, *After the Terror*, 2nd edn, Edinburgh University Press, 2003, pp. 51–58.

Ted Honderich, 'Our Omissions and Their Terrorism', in *Terrorism for Humanity: Inquiries in Political Philosophy*, Pluto Press, 2005.

Ted Honderich, 'The Principle of Humanity', in *Terrorism for Humanity: Inquiries in Political Philosophy*, Pluto Press, 2003.

Peter Singer, *One World: The Ethics of Globalization*, Yale University Press, 2005.

The Character of the Principle

Ted Honderich, *After the Terror*, 2nd edn, Edinburgh University Press, 2003, pp. 162–170.

The Strength of the Principle

Ted Honderich, *After the Terror*, 2nd edn, Edinburgh University Press, 2003.

The Ends and the Means Justify the Means

Ted Honderich, 'Consequentialism, Moralities of Concern, and Selfishness', in *On Political Means and Social Ends*, Edinburgh University Press, 2003.

Ted Honderich, *Punishment: The Supposed Justifications Revisited*, Pluto Press, 2005.

Burleigh Taylor Wilkins, *Terrorism and Collective Responsibility*, Routledge, 1992.

Defining Terrorism

Eqbal Ahmad, *Terrorism: Theirs and Ours*, Seven Stories Press, 2001.

J. Angelo Corlett, *Terrorism: A Philosophical Analysis*, Kluwer, 2003.

Terry Eagleton, *Holy Terror*, Oxford University Press, 2005.

Ted Honderich, 'On Democratic Terrorism', in *Terrorism for Humanity: Inquiries in Political Philosophy*, Pluto Press, 2003.

Igor Primoratz (ed.), *Terrorism: The Philosophical Issues*, Palgrave Macmillan, 2004.

John R. Rowan (ed.), *War and Terrorism*, Vol. 20 of *Social Philosophy Today*, Philosophy Documentation Center, 2004.

James P. Sterba (ed.), *Terrorism and International Justice*, Oxford University Press, 2003.

Palestine

Noam Chomsky, *Fateful Triangle: The United States, Israel and the Palestinians*, Pluto Press, 1999.

Norman G. Finkelstein, *Image and Reality of the Israel–Palestine Conflict*, 2nd edn, Verso, 2003.

David Hirst, *The Gun and the Olive Branch*, 2nd edn, Faber & Faber, 1984.

'Israel', *The World Guide, 2005–2006*, New Internationalist Publications, 2005.

Michael Neumann, *The Case Against Israel*, CounterPunch, 2005.

'Palestine', *The World Guide, 2005–2006*, New Internationalist Publications, 2005.

Ilan Pappe, *A History of Modern Palestine: One Land, Two Peoples*, Cambridge University Press, 2004.

Charles D. Smith, *Palestine and the Arab–Israeli Conflict: A History With Documents*, 5th edn, Bedford/St Martins, 2004.

Some Conclusions about Palestine

Ghada Karmi, *In Search of Fatima: A Palestinian Story*, Verso, 2004.

Michael Neumann, *The Case Against Israel*, CounterPunch, 2005.

Edward Said, *Out of Place: A Memoir*, Random House, 1999.

A Terrible Conclusion about Palestinian Terrorism

Virginia Held, 'Terrorism and War', *The Journal of Ethics*, 2004.

Ted Honderich, '*After the Terror*: A Book and Further Thoughts', *The Journal of Ethics*, 2005. Reprinted in 2nd edn of *After the Terror*.

Ted Honderich, 'Palestinian Terrorism, Morality, and Germany', *Rechtsphilosophische Hefte*, Band x, 2005.

Igor Primoratz, 'Terrorism in the Israeli–Palestinian Conflict: A Case Study in Applied Ethics', *Iygun: The Jerusalem Philosophical Quarterly*, 2006.

Saul Smilansky, 'Terrorism, Justification and Illusion', *Ethics*, 2004.

Understanding, Endorsing, Inciting

Geoffrey Stone, *Perilous Times: Free Speech in Wartime from the Sedition Act of 1798 to the War on Terrorism*, Norton & Co, 2004.

9/11

Anonymous American government author, *Through Our Enemies' Eyes: Osama Bin Laden, Radical Islam, and the Future of America*, Brasseys, 2002.

Paul Gilbert, *New Terror, New Wars*, Edinburgh University Press, 2003.

Ted Honderich, *After the Terror*, 2nd edn, Edinburgh University Press, 2003, pp. 89–115.

The 9/11 Commission Report: Final Report of the National Commission on Terrorist Attacks Upon the United States, Norton & Co, 2004.

9/11 and a Troubling Question

Ted Honderich, 'Consequentialism, Moralities of Concern, and Selfishness', in *On Political Means and Social Ends*, Edinburgh University Press, 2003.

Iraq

Noam Chomsky, *Hegemony or Survival: America's Quest for World Dominance*, Metropolitan Books, 2003.

Charles Tripp, *A History of Iraq*, Cambridge University Press, 2002.

Iraq Conclusions, Killing Innocents

Ted Honderich, 'Later Thoughts on Terrorism for Humanity', in *After the Terror*, 2nd edn, Edinburgh University Press, 2003, pp. 170–174.

George Monbiot, 'The Media are Minimizing U.S. and British War Crimes in Iraq', *Guardian*, 8 November 2005.

7/7 and the Importance of Horror

Ted Honderich, 'Hierarchic Democracy and the Necessity of Mass Civil Disobedience and Non-Cooperation', in *On Political Means and Social Ends*, Edinburgh University Press, 2003.

Ted Honderich, 'Wretchedness and Terrorism, and Differences We Make Between Them', in *Terrorism for Humanity: Inquiries in Political Philosophy*, Pluto Press, 2003.

7/7 and Who are the Enemies of this Terrorism?

Ted Honderich, *Conservatism: Burke, Nozick, Bush, Blair?*, Pluto Press, 2005, pp. 259–269, 203–311.

Simon Jenkins, 'This is an Act of Censorship Worthy of Joseph Goebbels', *Guardian*, 23 September 2005.

Corey Robin, *Fear: The History of a Political Idea*, Oxford University Press, 2004.

Our Societies and the War on Terror

Ted Honderich, *Conservatism: Burke, Nozick, Bush, Blair?*, Pluto Press, 2005.

Ted Honderich, *Punishment: The Supposed Justifications Revisited*, Pluto Press, 2005, pp. 201–216.

Uncertainty and the Effect of Not Judging

Ted Honderich, *After the Terror*, 2nd edn, Edinburgh University Press, 2003, pp. 121–124.

Postscript on Anti-Semitism

Ted Honderich, '*After the Terror*: A Book and Further Thoughts', in *On Political Means and Social Ends*, Edinburgh University Press, 2003.

'The Fall and Rise of a Book in Germany', Ted Honderich website, http://www.homepages.ucl.ac.uk/~uctytho/.

'Ted Honderich and the Newpaper London Student, and a Postscript', Ted Honderich website.

Ted Honderich, 'Palestinian Terrorism, Morality, and Germany', *Rechtsphilosophische Hefte*, Band x, 2005.

Brian Klug, 'The Collective Jew: Israel and the New Antisemitism', *Patterns of Prejudice*, June 2003.

Michael Neuman, 'What Is Anti-Semitism?', in Alexander Cockburn and Jeffrey St Clair (eds), *The Politics of Anti-Semitism*, Counterpunch and AK Press, 2003.

Paul de Rooij, 'Why Ted Honderich is Wrong on All Counts', *CounterPunch*, http://www.counterpunch.org/rooij02282005.html.

Index